Memories of

Express & Star
Wolverhampton Wanderers FC
Official Publication

Molineux

Memories of Molineux

Express & Star
Wolverhampton Wanderers FC
Official Publication

Express & Star

The Breedon Books
Publishing Company
Derby

First published in Great Britain by
The Breedon Books Publishing Company Limited
Breedon House, 44 Friar Gate, Derby, DE1 1DA.
1996

ISBN 1 85983 069 2

Printed and bound in England by Butler & Tanner Ltd.
Selwood Printing Works, Caxton Road, Frome, Somerset.

Colour separations by Colour Services, Wigston, Leicester.

Jackets printed by Lawrence-Allen, Weston-super-Mare, Avon.

Contents

Acknowledgments

The publishers wish to thank the following for their help in compiling this book: Graham Hughes, Wolverhampton Wanderers FC; Nigel Bond, Wednesfield; John Bolger, Wednesfield; Barry Cottis, Wolverhampton; Frances Cartwright, Wolverhampton; Brian Collins, Rugeley; F Evans, Willenhall; M Finlayson, Kingswinford; K Fellows, Coseley; Mr Poole, Wolverhampton; B Gamston, Dudley; Anthony Jones, Portobello; Malcolm Lloyd, Willenhall; Alan Mills, Walsall; Mr Umesh Patel, Wolverhampton; Gerry Russell, Wolverhampton; Miss G Rogers, Wolverhampton; Mr Randle, Stafford; Mrs L Smith, Wednesbury; Mrs Stanton, New Invention; Mr Till, Wolverhampton; Albert Ward, Walsall; H Till, Wolverhampton; Mr Baker, Wednesfield; M Constable, Wolverhampton; Mr M Powell, Wolverhampton; Mr Whitehead, Wolverhampton; Mr James Nicklin, Wolverhampton; Mr Joyce, Wolverhampton; Mrs Rochelle, Wolverhampton; Mr John Williams, Wednesfield; Mr L Perkins, Walsall; K W Deans, Lower Penn; Mrs Moorhouse, Wolverhampton; Mr Colin Allen, Walsall; R West, Stourbridge; Mr Knowles, Wolverhampton; Mrs L G Perkins, Walsall; Mr Frank Wedge, Wolverhampton; John Breakwell, Kingswinford; Mr D Potter, Stourbridge; T N Armet, Tettenhall; S T Cosnett, Wolverhampton; Mrs Jean Baker, Willenhall; Mrs A S Potts, Cannock; Mr Ron G Horton, Willenhall; Terry Hickman, Stourport; Mr Cooper, Wolverhampton; Mr Adams, Cannock; Mrs J Hipwell, Albrighton; Honourable Chuck Perry, Moxley; Mr T Stone, Wolverhampton; Jack Goodwin, Doxey; Mr J Timmins, Wolverhampton; Mr Lovatt, Wednesbury; Mrs M Barnes, Wolverhampton; F Matthews, Wednesfield; Harold Whitehouse, Finchfield; Mr Bailey, Wolverhampton; Gerry Russell, Wolverhampton; Mr C M Pearson, Wolverhampton; Mr J H Taylor, Wolverhampton; Mr Vic Hodgkiss, Wolverhampton; Mr Roger Jones, Willenhall; Mr Frank Munger, Castlecroft; Mr Craddock, Cannock; Mr Sadler, Wolverhampton; Mrs Rudkin, Wednesfield; Mr Whitehouse, Walsall; Mrs Betty Morris, Walsall; Heather Lewis, Wolverhampton; Dr H Wilkes, Wolverhampton; Mrs Gwendoline Lowndes, Hilton, Shropshire.

Introduction

When we started out on the long, but enjoyable task of researching material for this book, it was with the intention of bringing together in one publication the best of our vast archive of old Wolves pictures.

Deciding which pictures to leave out was no easy task - and was soon made worse for our researchers when one of them had a bright idea.

"Let's ask our own *Express & Star* readers if they have any memorabilia which might be suitable," she said.

Within days we were overwhelmed by the response as pictures, scrapbooks, records and cuttings flooded in. Some were collections built up over a lifetime and many readers asked us to keep them for future generations. We have a wonderful relationship with Wolves and it was decided to pass these to the club itself for possible inclusion in their own collection.

Since then, of course, we have also had the marvellous Billy Wright exhibition.

On behalf of everyone at the newspaper I would like to place on record my thanks to all those readers who donated material. We have included their names in the acknowledgement list and apologise in advance for any whose names many have been inadvertently omitted.

With the wealth of material still to be processed we are already looking at the possibility of a second book and their names will be recorded then.

Meanwhile I am sure you will have many happy hours studying the wonderful pictures in this journey through time.

Warren Wilson

Warren Wilson
Editor, *Express & Star*

The First 60 Years

Wolves 1887-style. This was the last year of Cup and friendly football only. In 1888, Wolves became founder-members of the Football League.

How Wolves lined up in 1904-05. Back row (left to right): J.Whitehouse, J.Jones, R.Betteley, C.Walker, T.Baddeley, W.Annis. Front row: A.Baynham, A.Haywood, W.Wooldridge, J.Smith, J.Miller.

Action from a League game between Wolves and Birmingham in 1905.

Wolves in 1905-06. Back row (left to right): A.Fletcher (trainer), T.Lunn, E.Juggins, T.Baddeley, J.Stanley, R.Betteley. Middle row: A.Baynham, J.Smith, W.Wooldridge, W.Layton, T.Reybould. Front row: E.James, H. Hughes, J.Whitehouse.

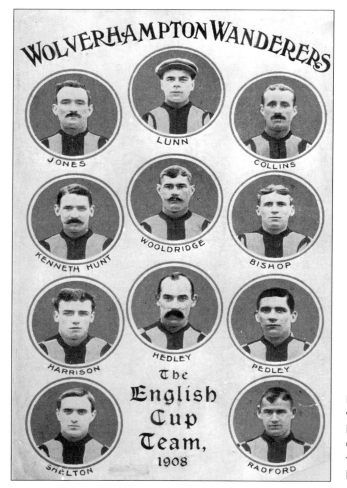

And a Wolves line-up in 1907-08. Back row (left to right): Shepherd, Evans, Barker, Jeffs, Fleming, Judson (assistant trainer). Middle row: Dr Wolverson, Lloyd, Jones, Wooldridge, Lunn, Collins, Bishop, Addenbrooke (secretary-manager). Front row: Harrison, Shelton, Hedley, Radford, Pedley. Inset: Revd Kenneth Hunt.

Presenting the 1908 FA Cup winners, victorious 3-1 against Newcastle in the Final at Crystal Palace thanks to goals from Hunt, Harrison and Hedley.

Thou shalt not pass. Wolves players fill the goalmouth before their opening game of the 1905-06 season, away to Nottingham Forest. From left: Albert Baynham, Jack Smith, Billy Wooldridge, Jackery Jones, Dick Betteley, Tom Baddeley, Arnold Henshall, Tom Raybould, Jack Whitehouse, Charlie Williams, Jack Hopkins.

When the Wolves were striped...another pre-World War One team group.

1920 Wolves. Back row (left to right): Jack Addenbrooke (secretary-manager), Dicky Baugh Jnr, Val Gregory, Teddy Peers, Maurice Woodward, Joe Hodnett, George Marshall. Front row: Billy Harrison, Arthur Potts, George Edmonds, Eric Cutler, Sammy Brooks.

Similar line-up, a year or two later, and a different kit.

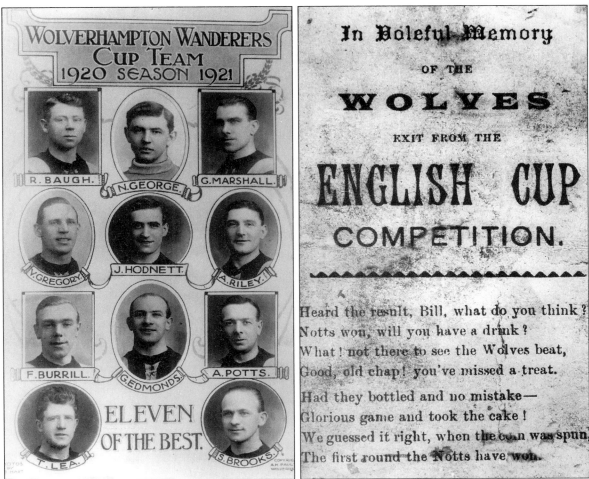

WOLVERHAMPTON WANDERERS
CUP TEAM
1920 SEASON 1921

R. BAUGH.   N. GEORGE.   G. MARSHALL.

V. GREGORY.   J. HODNETT.   A. RILEY.

F. BURRILL.   G. EDMONDS.   A. POTTS.

T. LEA.   ELEVEN OF THE BEST.   S. BROOKS.

In Doleful Memory

OF THE

WOLVES

EXIT FROM THE

ENGLISH CUP

COMPETITION.

Heard the result, Bill, what do you think?
Notts won, will you have a drink?
What! not there to see the Wolves beat,
Good, old chap! you've missed a treat.

Had they bottled and no mistake—
Glorious game and took the cake!
We guessed it right, when the coin was spun,
The first round the Notts have won.

Far left: The caption on this valuable keepsake almost says it all. But this Wolves side were actually beaten 1-0 in the 1920-21 FA Cup Final by Tottenham at Chelsea.

Left: Tactful mourning of a poor Cup result.

Match-day photo-call, 1921-22.

Harold Shaw (left) with former Wolves reserve player Frank Huband, the founder of Wolverhampton Amateur Boxing Club. Shaw, a Hednesford-born left-back, was the junior member of Wolves' team of Third Division North title-winners in 1923-24, playing nearly 250 games for the club before embarking on an eight-year career with Sunderland.

Wolves the 1923-24 Third Division North champions, together with club officials, having conquered teams like Ashington, Durham City and New Brighton along the way. Back row (left to right): J.Baker, A.Hoskins, E.Barker, T.Simpson, F.Hollins, H.Mills. Middle row: G.Jobey (manager), G.Holley (trainer), Albert Legge, Ben Timmins, Bill Caddick, Noel George, Albert Kay, Ted Watson, J.Davis, Oakley, Major A.Holloway. Front row: Tom Davison, Jack Harrington, Stuart McMillan, Tommy Bowen, Stan Fazackerley, George Getgood, Tom Phillipson, Harry Lees, Evan Edwards, Harry Shaw.

Over the top it goes from 'keeper Noel George, as Wolves battle to a goalless draw at The Valley against Charlton Athletic in the FA Cup second round tie in 1924. A lone Stan Fazackerley goal won them the replay at Molineux.

Wolves v Reading in October 1926. Boswell scores for Wolves.

Wolves line-up, mid-1920s.

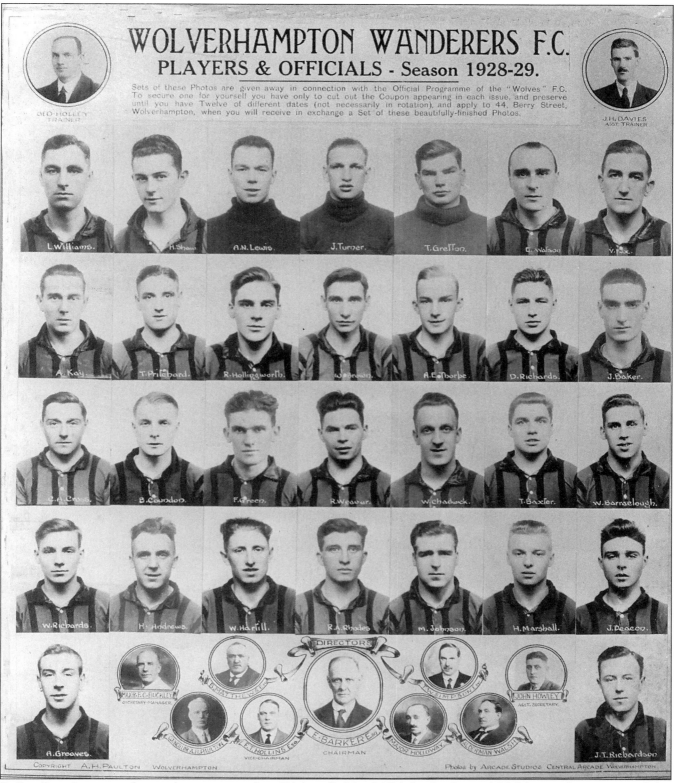

Roll-call at the start of an unhappy campaign. Wolves finished 17th in the Second Division and went out of the FA Cup at their first hurdle, at home to Mansfield.

WOLVERHAMPTON WANDERERS. *By "MATT"*

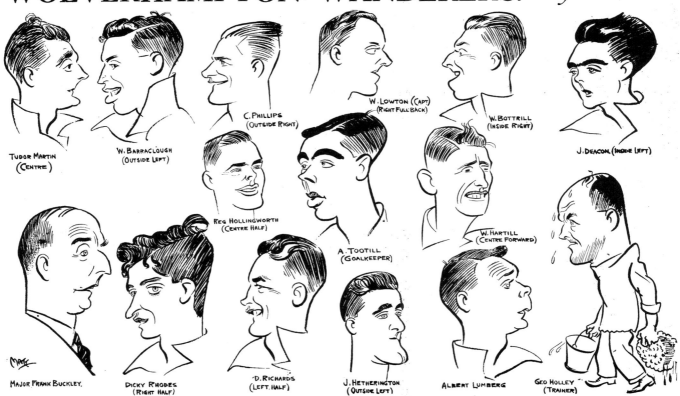

Artistic, caricature look at Wolves' squad at the start of the 1930s.

Billy Hartill, Wolves' leading goalscorer until John Richards came along, in action against Albion at Molineux in the early 1930s, with Harold Pearson, the Baggies goalkeeper, beating him to the ball.

Billy Hartill in action against Spurs at Molineux with visiting 'keeper Spiers fisting the ball clear as Poynton looks on. Spiers later joined Wolves.

A team with a tough act to follow. The Molineux Reserves in a season in which Wolves won the Second Division title under Major Frank Buckley, despite losing their final two games. Pictured are (back row from left): Bradford (trainer), Lax, J.Griffiths, Whittaker, Bellis, Smith. Front row: Crook, Connaboy, J.R.Griffiths, Buttery, Hetherington, Lumberg.

Finding their feet. After promotion from the Second Division in 1931-32, Wolves just stayed up by finishing 20th the following year and then, with this 1933-34 squad, they improved to 15th. Back row (left to right): J.Smith, W.Lowton, R.Hollingworth, F.Pincott, F.Wildman, C.Spiers, J.Ellis, J.Nelson, C.Shaw, R.Rhodes. Middle row: D.Richards, I.Harwood, W.Hartill, J.Preece, J.Dowen, W.Bucknall, J.Clayton, J.Gardiner, M.Burgin, T.Wildsmith. Front row: J.Deacon, S.Protheroe, T.Smalley, W.Bryant, C.Phillips, Major Frank Buckley (secretary-manager), W.Barraclough, J.Shelton, M.Crook, A.Hetherington, L.Heelbeck.

Delusions of Wembley. Wolves line up for the camera in 1934-35, but their journey in the FA Cup took them only to the fourth round and a 2-1 home defeat by Sheffield Wednesday. Back row (left to right): R.Rhodes, R.Hollingworth, J.Utterson, C.Shaw, J.Nelson, T.Smalley, D.Richards, A.Hetherington. Front row: J.Brown, C.Phillips, W.Hartill, D.Martin, B.Jones, M.Crook, W.Wrigglesworth.

Albert Kay, who achieved the distinction of helping Wolves win both the Third Division North in 1923-24 and the Second Division eight years later. This wing-half or full-back served the club for ten years before retiring to live on the outskirts of Wolverhampton.

Charlie Phillips, one of Wolves' Welsh international brigade.

Top, left: Cuthbert `Charlie' Phillips, a prolific forward who rattled in 65 goals in 202 senior Wolves appearances between 1929 and 1936. His efforts earned him 13 Welsh caps and also service with neighbours Aston Villa and Birmingham City.

Top, right: Dai Richards, a veteran of well over 200 matches for Wolves, at left-half or inside-forward, in a career that also took in Birmingham and Walsall before he retired to Sedgley. Capped 21 times by Wales.

Wilf Lowton, powerful penalty-specialist right-back who skippered Wolves for the first half of the 1930s, including their promotion campaign of 1931-32, when he missed only one League game.

Left: Billy Barraclough, another of the mainstays of Wolves' Second Division title-winning side of 1932. The outside-left scored 19 goals for the club in 183 senior games.

Right: Billy Hartill, third highest scorer in Wolves history, with 170 goals in only 234 outings between 1929 and 1935; a period that saw the club regain their top-flight status.

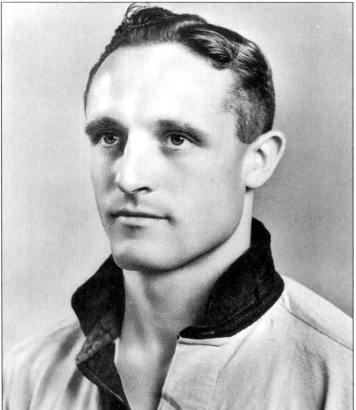

Above: Bill Morris; Handsworth-born central defender, who played for Wolves from 1933 to 1947. He made well over 250 first-team appearances before moving on to Dudley Town.

Bryn Jones, who became Britain's most expensive footballer when he moved from Molineux to Arsenal for £14,000 in 1938! The former pit worker spent five years with Wolves, appearing in 177 senior games and scoring 57 goals. His ball-playing brilliance also earned him 17 full caps for Wales in a career that would have brought him many more but for the war. His departure caused something of an outrage among Wolves fans.

Four big catches. From left: Stan Cullis, Tom Galley, Dennis Westcott and Dickie Dorsett.

Narrow escape for Albion in a 1930s Hawthorns derby against Wolves.

Wolves versus Notts County in the third round of the FA Cup on January 12, 1935. Wolves won 4-0 but went out in the next round at home to Sheffield Wednesday.

Wolves 3 Liverpool 1, November 16, 1935. Wolves finished 15th in this season but the Merseysiders provided them with rich pickings in the form of a League double.

On its way. A goal-bound shot during the England v Wales full international at Molineux in 1936. Wales, including Wolves' Bryn Jones, won 2-1 in front of a crowd of 22,613.

Wolves versus Arsenal, April 13, 1935 and a game that ended in a 1-1 draw, Bryn Jones (pictured here on the left) scoring for Wolves. He later signed for the Gunners.

Wolves 2 Villa 2, April 13, 1936. Three days earlier, Villa had won the clash of the two sides at Villa Park by a scoreline of 4-2, the two games attracting a combined attendance of nearly 100,000.

Right and below:
Wolves v Bolton, October 3, 1936, and a costly 3-2 defeat for Major Buckley's men. They finished the season fifth.

Wolves v Villa again at Molineux.

Molineux on FA Cup semi-final day. Sheffield United beat Fulham 2-1 in this last-four clash in the 1935-36 competition.

Wolves v Goodyear, September 1936, at the opening of Wingfoot Park. Wolves won 4-1, with Waring, Wrigglesworth and Wright (2) scoring. The team was: Weare, Mitchell, Shaw, Dorsett, Mordue, Lottam, Wrigglesworth, Keely, Waring, Wright and Rawley. Note the gentleman on the second row back, far right.

Molineux tragedy. Wolves players act as coffin-bearers and others form a solemn guard of honour as the body of goalkeeper Jimmy Utterson is carried to its final resting place in 1936. The player, who appeared in 14 first-team games for the club before a terminal illness, was briefly carried back to the ground after his death as a mark of respect.

Pre-season photo-call a couple of years before World War Two. Stan Cullis and Tom Galley are side-by-side at the right-hand end of the second row from the back.

Wolves versus Manchester City in the first match of the 1937-38 campaign. The Wolves won 3-1 thanks to a Gordon Clayton hat-trick.

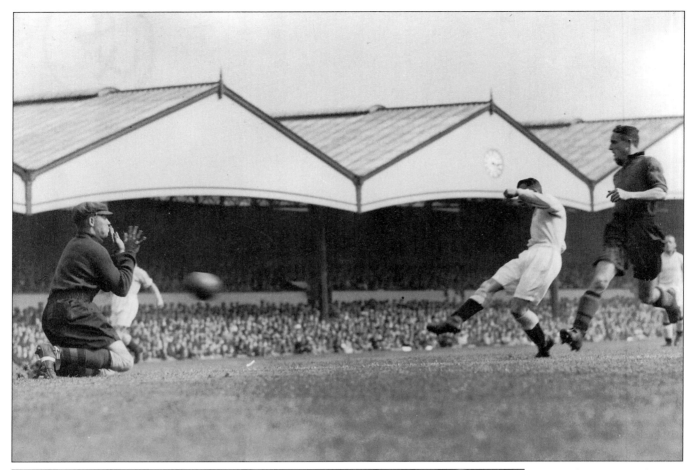

Wolves v Manchester City again, marked here by an anxious moment for Wolves 'keeper Alex Scott.

Tense moments as Wolves skipper Stan Cullis and his Sunderland counterpart Raich Carter toss up before the second replay of the 1937 FA Cup quarter-final at Hillsborough. The Wearsiders won 4-0 and went on to lift the trophy.

Banquet time at Wolves, October 20, 1937. It was the year Wolves celebrated their 60th anniversary.

Major Frank Buckley; manager of Wolves even longer (by a year) than Cullis. The former Aston Villa youngster held the reins from 1927 to 1944, lifting them from Second Division obscurity to a place close to the summit of the English game. His side were shock losers of the 1939 FA Cup Final against Portsmouth but the foundations for later glories were being laid.

Harry Thompson and Tom Smalley, who made a combined total of 269 appearances for Wolves in the second half of the 1930s, almost 200 of them by Smalley.

Joe Gardiner, later to become the club's veteran trainer, and Teddy Maguire, a late '30s team-mate.

Bill Morris, 197 senior Wolves appearances from the war-interrupted 1933 to 1947 period.

March 17, 1937, and Wolves play out their second 1-1 draw of the season with Portsmouth, this time beneath the shadow of the unmistakable Molineux Street Stand.

More action from the Wolves v Portsmouth draw on March 17, 1937, watched in appalling conditions by a meagre 6,113 crowd.

FA Cup fourth-round success for Wolves as they push towards victory in a 2-1 replay win at Bramall Lane on February 4, 1937. The run took them to the sixth round, where they lost in a second replay to Sunderland.

Aerial action in the Brentford goalmouth in Wolves' 2-0 win over the Londoners on January 29, 1938. Wolves finished runners-up in the championship race both that season and 12 months later.

Bert Barlow, who made three appearances for Wolves, all in 1938-39. Then he moved on to Portsmouth and won an FA Cup winners' medal the same season, helping his new club beat his old 4-1 in the Final.

On the rampage. Billy Hartill puts his man under pressure. Note the referee's attire.

Wolves run amok in their game versus Everton on February 13, 1937, winning 7-2 thanks to four goals by Clayton, two by Galley and one from Ashall.

Wolves held by Sunderland on March 6, 1937, in a 1-1 draw in the quarter-final of the FA Cup. The Wearsiders went through in a second replay.

Goalless deadlock between Wolves and Preston on April 18, 1938. Pictured are Preston goalkeeper Holdcroft and Wolves attackers Dorsett, Westcott and Wright (nearest camera).

Joe Gardiner and Stan Cullis line up for the Football League side against the Scottish League team at Molineux in the 1930s. It is one of three inter-League games to have been played at the ground, the English side winning this meeting 3-1 in front of a 28,389 crowd on November 2, 1938. Back row (left to right): Greenhalgh (Everton), Mercer (Everton), Gardiner (Wolves), Woodley (Chelsea), Davies (trainer, Wolves), Lawton (Everton). Front row: Boyes (Everton), Dix (Derby), Sproston (Tottenham), Cullis (Wolves), Hall (Tottenham), Matthews (Stoke).

Wolves, pictured in the late 1930s.

Wolves' squad in the late 1930s. Back row (left to right): C.Spiers, D.Waker, T.Anderson, C.Sidlow, A.Tye, A.Scott, J.Jones, T.Shield, D.Thornhill, W.Wright, C.Caine. Middle row: J.Crump, C.Tucker, J.Archer, J.Cringan, D.Parker, J.Rooney, E.Robinson, H.Wright, A.McMahon, R.Goddard, A.Steen, F.Rawcliffe. Front row: J.Davis (Trainer), S.Burton, W.Morris, T.Galley, D.Westcott, S.Cullis, T.Taylor, A.McIntosh, D.Dorsett, J.Gardiner, J.Maguire, J.Mullen.

It's Arsenal v Wolves, but guess the year and the competition! This obscure occasion was an April 1938 clash for the Mayor of Colchester's Cup at Layer Road. Wolves won 1-0 in front of 17,584 against a side containing the famous Compton brothers.

Off to Wembley, but it wasn't to prove a happy occasion. Wolves' 1939 FA Cup Final side line up at Molineux before their 4-1 defeat against Portsmouth. Back row (left to right): Tom Galley, Bill Morris, Stan Cullis, Alex Scott, Frank Taylor, Joe Gardiner. Front row: Stan Burton, Alex McIntosh, Dennis Westcott, Dickie Dorsett, Teddy Maguire. The outbreak of the war ensured this was the club's last FA Cup game for seven seasons.

1939 again, but this time including Jimmy Mullen, who didn't play in that Wembley Final. Back row (left to right): Bill Morris, Tom Galley, Alex Scott, Frank Taylor, Joe Gardiner. Front row: Jimmy Mullen, Stan Burton, Alex McIntosh, Stan Cullis, Dennis Westcott, Dickie Dorsett, Teddy Maguire.

Sign here please. The seated Stan Cullis (left) and Dickie Dorsett lead their team-mates in the ritual autograph session

Lucky mascot? Sadly not! Jimmy Mullen and skipper Stan Cullis clutch a furry friend for luck in the build-up to the 1939 FA Cup Final. The side were nevertheless beaten emphatically by Portsmouth.

Wolves at Wembley — Part 1

1939 FA Cup Final

Portsmouth 4
Wolves 1

Proud moment for Wolves' players as they are introduced to King George VI before taking on Portsmouth in the 1939

A Cup Final at Wembley. Full-back Bill Morris is the man being introduced here to the monarch by skipper Stan Cullis.

Never mind, there's always next year. But there wasn't. This Wolves side, beaten 4-1 by Portsmouth at Wembley, had to wait seven seasons, thanks to the war, to play in the FA Cup again.

WOLVERHAMPTON WANDERERS

MORRIS   SCOTT   TAYLOR

GALLEY   CULLIS   GARDINER

McINTOSH   WESTCOTT   DORSETT

BURTON   MAGUIRE

The English Cup Team, 1939

Cup Final greeting for Wolves manager Major Frank Buckley from King George VI.

Parker scores Portsmouth's fourth goal.

An important block from Wolves number-five Stan Cullis, with 'keeper Alex Scott out of position in the FA Cup Final defeat on April 29, 1939.

FA Cup Final 1939; Dorsett scores Wolves' only goal.

Pompey 'keeper Walker clears under pressure from Wolves' Dennis Westcott.

Wartime and Beyond

The Boys And—
Mullen	Outside-left
Gardiner	Left-back
Dowen	Full-back
Taylor	Right-back
Sidlow	Goalkeeper
Scott	Goalkeeper
Morris	Right-back
Parker	Full-back
Goddard	Right-half
Steen	Outside-right
R. Bainbridge	

WOLVES 1939-40

—Their Position
Cullis	Centre-h...
Galley	Centre-h...
Bainbridge	Half-ba...
Brown	Full-ba...
H. Wright	Inside forwa...
McIntosh	Inside-ri...
Westcott	Centre-forwa...
McMahon	Centre-forwa...
Dorsett	Inside-l...
Thornhill	Left-h...
W. Wright	Wing forwa...

Many of Wolves' 1939 Wembley side at the start of the following Football League campaign; the one cut down in its infancy upon the outbreak of World War Two.

CRISIS...

WESTCOTT AGAIN IN SCORING MOOD

TWO FIRST-HALF GOALS AT MEADOW-LANE

RAYNOR REPLIES FOR NOTTS

By a Special Correspondent

Notts County provided Wolves with their second war-time friendly match at Meadow-lane, Nottingham, today.

This was the first time Wolves have visited the ground since April, 1932.

Wolves were minus several of their first team members, but fielded a strong eleven. Read, a half-back, led the Notts attack. The attendance at the start numbered about 4,000. Teams:—

NOTTS COUNTY.—Flower; Mills, Chester; Buckley, Barke, Weightman, Houghton, Rayner, Read, Cooper, Towler.

WOLVES.—Sidlow; Brown, Taylor; Goddard, Galley, Rawcliffe; Morris, McIntosh, Westcott, Wright (H.), Wright (W.).

Referee: M. G. Tucker (Nottingham).

Wolves won the toss, and Westcott sent Wright (W.) away. Mills, however, neatly intervened.

Galley was prominent, and from one of his passes Westcott was held up only with difficulty.

In a Notts attack Houghton sent in a hard drive, the ball striking Sidlow and bouncing across the goal, Brown clearing. The Notts defenders, particularly Weightman, showed good judgment when Morris and McIntosh looked dangerous.

Westcott used both wings cleverly, and Morris sent in a fine centre which Barke headed.

From a corner well placed by Wright (W.), Flower punched the ball off Westcott's head.

Play was fairly keen, and Goddard played a determined game against the Cooper-Towler wing.

Barke neatly intercepted a dangerous movement by Westcott and McIntosh. Flower completing the clearance.

Houghton missed a good chance for Notts when Raynor beat Galley and Taylor...

WESTCOTT, scored three goals against Albion last week and two more in the first half against Notts County today.

FRIENDLY MATCH HALF-TIMES

NOTTS COUNTY 1, WOLVES 2	
Albion 2, Stoke 0.	
Alloa 0, Stenhousemuir 0.	
Aldershot 0, An Army XI. 1.	
Ayr 0, Kilmarnock 0.	
Barnsley 1, Newcastle United 0.	
Barrow 2, Carlisle 2.	
Blackpool 1, Bolton 0.	
Bournemouth 1, Torquay 0.	
Bradford 1, Grimsby 0.	
Bradford City 1, Doncaster 0.	
Brentford 1, Crystal Palace 0.	
Brighton 0, Southampton 0.	
Burnley 1, Bury 3.	
Celtic 1, Queen's Park 1.	
Chelmsford 1, Charlton 1.	
Chester 2, Wrexham 1.	
Chesterfield 1, Huddersfield 0.	
Coventry 0, Leicester 1.	
Darlington 1, Hartlepools 1.	
Dundee Utd. 1, St. Jo...	
...Preston	

Stoke Clev... But Albi... Had Pun...

By Dem...

Not more than 3,000 sp... start of West Bromwich... with Stoke City at the Hawthor...

Saunders took the place of A... Albion goal, otherwise the sid... same as that defeated by Wolve...

Matthews was absent from... team, Peppitt playing on the ex... He was partnered by Antonio,... ton moved to inside-left. Ma... unable to leave his work in tim...

The teams were:—

ALBION.—Saunders; White, ... key, Cripton, McNab;... Banks, Jones (H. J.), Con... son.

STOKE CITY.—Martin; Bra... ham; Massey, Moult, S... Antonio, Sale, Ormston, ...

Referee, S. E. Law.

Albion opened well on the lef... drove against the bar. From ... Jones volleyed over.

Stoke went away beautifully... and Peppitt squared the bal... Sale to drive straight at Sa... held a fierce drive from the S... forward immediately afterwar...

The crowd, which had incre... saw some excellent football fro...

Jones (H. J.) worked his... to give his namesake a grea... Jones (E.) drove fiercely... after only nine minutes pl...

An interchange of position... and Banks enabled the latt... Harry Jones headed in, but ...

Another finely worked ... Connelly a chance, but the ... taking the ball on the run, s... high.

Albion were doing most of ... but their finishing was not t... positional work being at fa... inside men were erratic in s... Banks worked a good open... Jones, who, having elude... centre-half, sliced weakly to ...

A clever close-passing mo... Stoke forwards caused tro... position was relieved by Sh... had put wide.

The football on both side... with Stoke having the b... understanding.

The Albion defence, howe... Peppitt made a gr...

A report of Wolves' wartime game at Notts County in 1939 — Billy Wright's debut.

53

Above: Stan Cullis shakes hands with Matt Busby, the man on whom he modelled himself as a player, before a Scotland v England wartime international.

Wedding day for the happy Cullises.

Stan Cullis; an outstanding player with Wolves from 1934 to 1947 and then their manager for 16 memorable years, highlighted by the winning of three Football League championships, the FA Cup twice, the Charity Shield, the FA Youth Cup and the Central League title. He also played 12 full games for England, as well as many wartime internationals, and represented the Football League.

1930s' and 1940s' goal sensation Dennis Westcott, who could have compiled a tally of Steve Bull proportions had it not been for World War Two. His total of 124 in 144 appearances was boosted by more than 90 more in wartime football, his haul of 43 in 1938-39 standing as a seasonal best for 49 seasons until Bull struck gold.

Ready for action. Wolves face the camera before a wartime game against Albion at The Hawthorns. During the 1939-45 hostilities, the club played more than 250 matches after the start of Hitler's march through Europe had caused League football to be suspended following only three games of the 1939-40 campaign.

Diminutive Norman Deeley in 1948. He would later become a Wolves Cup Final hero, figure in two First Division championship-winning sides and win two England caps.

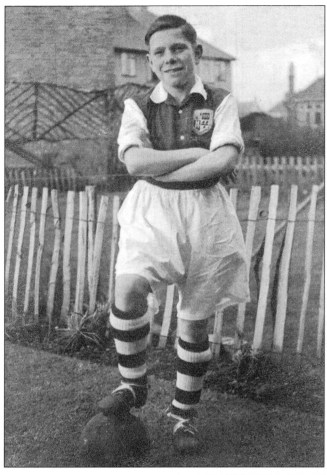

Willie Forbes heads Wolves' goal in a 2-1 home defeat by Liverpool in December 1947.

Opening day of the 1947-48 season. Sammy Smyth jumps for the ball as Manchester City number-two Bert Sproston watches and Wolves' number-eight Jesse Pye looks on. Wolves lost 4-3 at Maine Road.

Manchester City v Wolves in 1947. Johnny Hancocks drives in Wolves' first goal of the new season.

Look closely at this picture and there's an important omission — one of Wolves' players! Billy Crook was temporarily absent for this 1948 shot as Angus McLean, Bill Shorthouse, Bert Williams, Roy Pritchard, Jesse Pye, Billy Wright, Sammy Smyth, Willie Forbes, Jimmy Mullen and Johnny Hancocks form a pre-match line-up.

Johnny Hancocks in action against Blackpool in January 1948.

Dennis Westcott takes on Villa's Frank Moss in a 1948 clash.

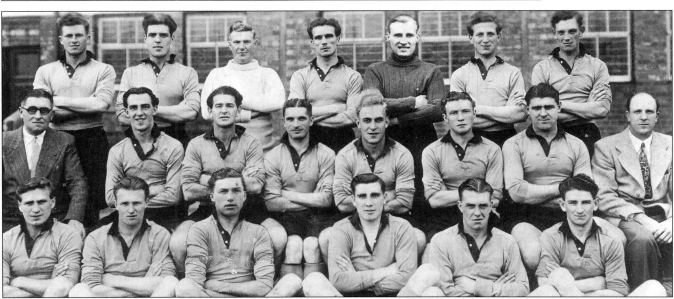

Now it's Cullis the manager as Wolves line up in the late-1940s. Back row (left to right): Terry Springthorpe, Lol Kelly, Jack Davies (trainer), Alex Simpson, Bert Williams, Sammy Smyth, Bill Baxter. Middle row: Jack Howley (secretary), Willie Forbes, Jesse Pye, Johnny Hancocks, Billy Wright, Les Smith, Angus McLean, Stan Cullis (manager). Front row: Jimmy Mullen, Jimmy Dunn, Billy Crook, Bill Shorthouse, Les Mynard, Roy Pritchard.

The 1949 FA Cup Final squad. Alf Crook (second from right) and Laurie Kelly (third from the right) were the two who did not get chosen for Wembley.

One of Wolves' epic games, the 1949 FA Cup semi-final replay at Goodison. Bert Williams saves from Manchester United's Jimmy Delaney as Alf Crook watches.

Wolves at Wembley — Part 2

1949 FA Cup Final

Wolves 3
Leicester City 1

Sporting Star. Saturday. April 30, 1949

MITCHELLS
"Good Honest Beer"
BUTLERS

Sporting Star
CUP SPECIAL

No. 710   WOLVERHAMPTON, SATURDAY, APRIL 30, 1949   PRICE 1½d.

PLATE SHEET GLASS, PAINTS, OILS. Colours of all descriptions

★ **J. Edwards** (Wolverhampton) Ltd.
16, CLEVELAND STREET & BELL STREET, W hampton

IT'S OURS!

F.A. Cup Final: Wolves 3 Leicester City 1

WOLVES — Williams; Pritchard, Springthorpe; Crook (W.), Shorthouse, Wright (captain); Hancocks, Smyth, Pye, Dunn, Mu... (manager).

The 1949 Cup Final.
Billy Wright watches as Bert Williams turns a Leicester effort around the post.

A special old gold edition of the Sporting Star carried news of the 1949 Cup triumph.

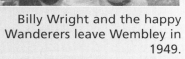

Billy Wright and the happy Wanderers leave Wembley in 1949.

Time to celebrate at a banquet after winning the Cup in 1949. Left to right are Jesse Pye, Billy Wright, Sammy Smyth and manager Stan Cullis.

We won the Cup! Skipper Billy Wright is chaired from the Wembley pitch by Bill Shorthouse and Jesse Pye after

the 3-1 defeat of Leicester.

Wolverhampton mayor Ted Lane welcomes Billy Wright and his 1949 FA Cup winners.

The 1949 Cup-winners. Back row (left to right): Billy Crook, Roy Pritchard, Bert Williams, Bill Shorthouse, Terry Springthorpe. Front row: Johnny Hancocks, Sammy Smyth, Stan Cullis (manager), Billy Wright, Jesse Pye, Jimmy Dunn, Jimmy Mullen.

Home with the FA Cup — Billy Wright with the trophy to show to the crowd before the League game against Preston two days later.

Those Glorious 1950s

August 26, 1950. Wolves line up at Craven Cottage where they lost 2-1 to Fulham. Back row (left to right): Billy Crook, Roy Pritchard, Ray Chatham, Bert Williams, Roy Swinbourne, Angus McLean. Front row: Jimmy Dunn, John Walker, Billy Wright, Jesse Pye, Jimmy Mullen.

Some of those who fell by the wayside. George Showell (third along back row) and Norman Deeley (with ball at his feet) made it from this 1950s Wolves junior side. But, despite the management of Stan Cullis, most fell short of the grade.

Wolves and England goalkeeper Bert Williams with inside-forward Ron Stockin. The latter joined Cardiff in 1955 and scored the Welsh side's only goal when Wolves equalled the First Division's biggest away win with a 9-1 triumph at Ninian Park.

A panoramic view of Molineux in its 1950s heyday, bursting to the seams as Jimmy Mullen takes on the Burnley defence.

Anxiety in the goalmouth as Bert Williams (hidden behind Len Duquemin and Wolves defenders), led here by the aerial Bill Shorthouse, deals with a Tottenham cross at White Hart Lane. Wolves won this December 1953 clash 3-2 on their way to winning the First Division title.

Shorthouse in control again as he slides the ball off the toe of Spurs' Len Duquemin in the same game.

The squad who brought the First Division title to Molineux in 1953-54. Back row (left to right): Slater, Pritchard, Flowers, Stuart, Williams, Shorthouse, Guttridge, Sims, Gibbons, Stockin, Clamp. Front row: Deeley, Smith, Broadbent, Swinbourne, Wright, Hancocks, Wilshaw, Mullen, Short.

Peter Broadbent is beaten by an unlikely goalkeeper, Jimmy Glazzard of Huddersfield, their centre-forward, who took over in goal when Jack Wheeler was injured 15 minutes from time as Wolves won 4-0 on Easter Monday, 1954, virtually to clinch the First Division championship for the first time in the club's history.

Blackpool's England full-back Tom Garrett tussles with Les Smith at Molineux in September 1954.

The final League game of 1954 which saw Wolves beat Spurs 2-0 to win the title — Jimmy Mullen features in this heading duel with a young Peter Baker, destined to be a member of Tottenham's 1961 Double-winning side. Left are Roy Swinbourne and Spurs' Bill Nicholson.

One of the club's all-time greats, Ron Flowers, in his early days at Molineux. He played over 500 first-team games for the club and won 49 England caps and, like Stan Cullis and Billy Wright before him, also skippered his country.

Above, left: Les Smith, one of the bit-part players during the golden era. In nine years with the club, he made only 94 first-team outings, but his 24 goals from the wings said much about his abilities and he played in the famous win over Honved.

Above, right: Roy Swinbourne, 114 goals in 230 Wolves appearances and in full flow until injury cruelly cut short his career in the mid-1950s.

Dennis Wilshaw, Wolves and England. He scored 112 goals in 219 appearances and also played for Walsall and Stoke City.

No time for frills. With Bert Williams off his line, Billy Wright applies the big boot to put paid to a Huddersfield attack at Molineux in April 1954. This 4-0 win left Wolves on the brink of lifting the title and they duly pipped Albion to the crown.

Wolves v Arsenal in the mid 1950s. Roy Swinbourne challenges but the Gunners' Welsh international 'keeper Jack Kelsey collects.

September 3, 1955. Cardiff 1 Wolves 9. Roy Swinbourne (number-nine) backheels Wolves' sixth as they set about equalling the First Division's biggest away win.

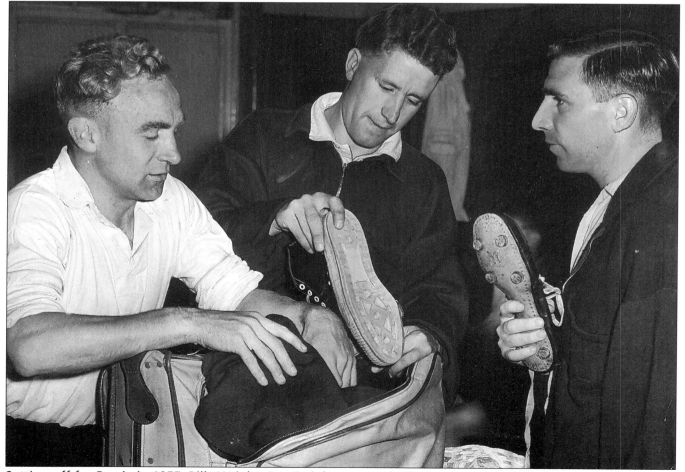

Setting off for Russia in 1955. Billy Wright, Roy Swinbourne and Bill Shorthouse pack their kit.

Dennis Wilshaw causes confusion in Chelsea's defence at Stamford Bridge in the 3-3 draw in October 1956. The Stoke-born forward once scored four goals for England against Scotland at Wembley as the highlight of an international career that brought him 12 full caps.

Another Chelsea-Wolves encounter in the late 1950s. Full-back Gerry Harris clears, watched by Bill Slater in the background, as Chelsea press.

January 26, 1957. Wolves lose 1-0 at home to lowly Bournemouth — the day the goalpost broke at Molineux's South Bank end.

Roger Byrne of Manchester United, one of the victims of the Munich Air Disaster in 1958, turns his back as Ron Flowers fires on goal during the meeting at Molineux in March 1957.

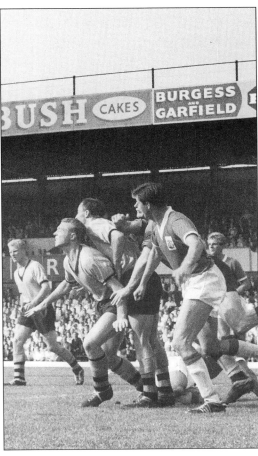

Wolves v Blues at St Andrew's. Finlayson fists clear with little respect for team-mates Eddie Clamp and George Showell, who end up looking decidedly groggy afterwards.

Three who played a big part in Wolves' successive First Division title wins in 1957-58 and 1958-59. Left to right: Ron Flowers, Malcolm Finlayson and Peter Broadbent.

Wolves' playing staff in 1958 after their efforts had won every trophy for which they competed, apart from the FA Cup.

The Wolves side who won the FA Youth Cup in 1958, beating Chelsea 6-1 in the return leg at Molineux after losing the first 5-1 at Stamford Bridge. Manager Stan Cullis is flanked by Phil Kelly (on his right) and Cliff Durandt. Extreme right on the front row is Ted Farmer who scored four goals in the Molineux game.

One of Wolves' finest goalkeepers, Malcolm Finlayson, turns a shot over the bar at Luton in November 1958.

February 1958. Wolves are on their way to a second First Division title with a 5-1 home win over Birmingham. Jimmy Murray (right) heads past 'keeper Gil Merrick. Racing back is Blues' former England defender Jeff Hall.

February 1958. Wolves beat Darlington 6-1 in the FA Cup at Molineux. Jimmy Murray heads in after a flick on from Norman Deeley.

The 1958-59 first-team squad and collection of trophies.

In October 1958, defender George Showell was tried at centre-forward and here he heads a goal in a 3-1 home win over Birmingham.

March 1959. Wolves put paid to one of their title rivals, Arsenal, 6-1 at Molineux and here Mick Lill slots in the third. Immediately behind him is Tommy Docherty, later to have a brief spell as manager of Wolves.

Peter Broadbent in scoring action again, driving the ball past Albert Dunlop of Everton at Molineux in September 1959.

Unhappy day for Wright, Slater, Finlayson, Stuart and Co. Beaten 6-2 at Chelsea on August 30, 1958, with a certain Jimmy Greaves scoring five of them.

Eddie Stuart leads out Wolves for the 1959 Charity Shield match against Nottingham Forest at Molineux. He is followed by Malcolm Finlayson and Gwyn Jones. Stuart had succeeded Billy Wright as skipper.

A Wolves reserve line-up in April 1959. Back row (left to right): Kirkham, Stobart, Mullen, Jones, Sidebottom, Kelly, Cocker, Jack Dowen (trainer). Front row: Mannion, Thomson, Showell, Durandt, Jackson, Horne.

The Nice party arrive at Wolverhampton station to sunshine and a warm welcome.

Performing the Niceties. Wolves skipper Wilf Lowton greets his counterpart from the visiting Nice side in a Molineux friendly in 1933.

Next page, top: The Frenchmen emerge from Molineux's famous old tunnel.

Bottom: End of a fabulous night, Eddie Stuart gets a handshake from the great Ferenc Puskas as the players leave the field following Wolves' famous 3-2 floodlit win over Honved to restore English football pride after the national side had lost 6-3 and 7-1 to the Magical Magyars.

Jimmy Mullen unleashes a fierce shot at goal during Wolves' 2-1 win over Moscow Dynamo in another of Molineux's famous floodlit friendlies of the mid-1950s.

Close shave for Dynamo. Mullen and Dennis Wilshaw follow up as a Bill Slater shot threatens to inflict further damage on the Russians' goalkeeper Lev Yashin.

The night the famous Real Madrid dropped in on Molineux. Eddie Stuart ushers a ball safely back to 'keeper Malcolm Finlayson on the famous occasion Wolves beat the reigning European Cup holders 3-2 in front of a crowd of 55,169 on October 17, 1957. The crack Spaniards included Di Stefano, Gento and Santamaria in their line-up and were held to a 2-2 draw by Stan Cullis's side in their own stadium a few weeks later.

Wolves in European Cup action. Peter Broadbent heads a spectacular goal in the 2-2 draw with Schalke 04 at Molineux in November 1958. Wolves lost the second leg 2-1 in Germany.

Mike Bailey exchanges pennants before Wolves' return to Europe – the 1971-72 UEFA Cup clash with Academica Coimbra. The visiting captain is Vasco Gervasio, the referee is Istvan Zsolt and Wolves went through 7-1 on aggregate.

John Richards slips the ball past goalkeeper Melo in the 3-0 home win over Academica Coimbra of Portugal as Wolves start their 1971-72 UEFA Cup campaign.

Derek Dougan scores the third goal against Academica in September 1971. Dougan scored three as Wolves went on to triumph 4-1 in the second leg in Portugal making an aggregate score of 7-1. Wolves went on to reach the Final where they lost to Spurs.

A Legend Called Billy

The young hopeful. William Ambrose Wright, aged eighteen and a half.

Lodger and landlady. Billy Wright and the homely Mrs Colley, with whom he lived in Tettenhall in his formative Molineux years.

Not just a fine footballer. The legendary Billy Wright shows a stylish touch on the bowls green too at Wingfoot Park, the Goodyear sports ground.

And this is how I do it. The master demonstrates to young Brian Mills, an admiring pupil from Bloxwich's Elmore Green High School, the style that won more than a century of England caps.

Billy Wright, without doubt, the most famous player in Wolves' history, leads out the team.

Comparing notes. Long-time Wolves coach Sammy Chung (left), also later the club's manager, consults with Billy Wright.

Now, son, I want you to be my captain. A congratulatory handshake to Billy Wright from Stan Cullis, another of the most famous names in Molineux history.

Billy Wright always had time to sign an autograph.

Tears in memory of a hero. For several weeks, Wolves fans paid their respects to Billy Wright CBE after his death in September 1994. Molineux was awash with hundreds of wreaths on its forecourt and it was soon decided that a statue should be erected on the site in tribute to of the club's greatest-ever footballer.

Elegance and balance from Wolves' finest-ever footballer; the much-loved and sadly-missed Billy Wright.

Wolves at Wembley — Part 3

1960 FA Cup Final

Wolves 3
Blackburn Rovers 0

Sporting Star

No. 1122
Telephone 22233
WOLVERHAMPTON, SATURDAY, MAY 7, 1960
PRICE 2½d

GLAZING
EDWARDS
CLEVELAND STREET
Wolverhampton

Vaux for Value
Don Everall LTD
for Vauxhalls

OURS AGAIN

3, BLACKBURN 0 — Attendance 100,000 ; Receipts £49,816

McGRATH (own goal), DEELEY (2).

DEELEY'S GOALS SETTLED IT

THE TWO IN ONE PICTURE

The 1960 FA Cup Final. Bill Slater introduces his side to the Duke of Gloucester. Ron Flowers is the player shaking hands, with Barry Stobart on his right and Eddie Clamp on his left.

A gold edition — the club switched colours in 1954 — to mark the Cup's return to Wolverhampton.

Malcolm Finlayson looks dazed after an early clash and gets some help from referee Kevin Howley.

Norman Deeley scores in the second half.

Wolves take the lead. Grounded Mick McGrath of Blackburn has turned Barry Stobart's cross into his own net and Norman Deeley joins the ball there, too.

Norman Deeley watches the ball enter the net for the first goal.

Harry Leyland can't prevent Deeley scoring again.

Jimmy Murray hits the deck with Blackburn centre-half Matt Woods.

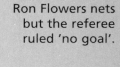

Ron Flowers nets but the referee ruled 'no goal'.

Harry Leyland gets the ball between leaping Wolves men Peter Broadbent (10) and Jimmy Murray (9).

Bill Slater
collects the Cup.

A pat on the head for
skipper Slater.

Bill Slater hoists aloft the trophy as he is chaired by Ron Flowers and Peter Broadbent.

Sporting Blackburn and England skipper Ronnie Clayton congratulates Wolves on their victory.

Eddie Clamp and Bill Slater parade the Cup around Wembley with Norman Deeley in hot pursuit.

Didn't we do well? Manager Stan Cullis discusses the game with Bill Slater in the dressing-room.

Manager Stan Cullis arrives at the celebration banquet. Behind him is Bobby Mason, who was not chosen for the big match at Wembley.

Happy Mr and Mrs George Showell toast success at the victory banquet.

The 1960s and into the '70s

Ted Farmer scores against Fulham at Craven Cottage in November 1960. In his first 27 League games, Farmer scored 28 goals. No player has made his debut in the top flight and had a better start.

Jimmy Murray and Ted Farmer in action against Chelsea on New Year's Eve, 1960. Murray is scoring one of his three goals past Peter Bonetti. Looking on is John Sillett, later to manage Coventry to an FA Cup triumph and then become a TV pundit.

Early TV days at Molineux — an ATV camera crew for a game in 1960.

Wolves in the 1960 FA Cup Final strip. Back row (left to right): Barry Stobart, Eddie Clamp, Gerry Mannion, Malcolm Finlayson, Geoff Sidebottom, George Showell, Gerry Harris. Front row: Norman Deeley, Des Horne, Jimmy Murray, Peter Broadbent, Bobby Mason. Sidebottom, Mannion and Mason were not chosen for Wembley. Missing from the side who beat Blackburn are skipper Bill Slater and Ron Flowers who were with the England team for the game against Scotland.

In control again. Malcolm Finlayson touches a corner to safety as right-back George Showell patrols one of the posts in the 3-0 FA Cup Final win over Blackburn Rovers in 1960.

Norman Deeley on the attack against Sheffield Wednesday. Hillsborough's famous cantilever stand can be seen still under construction in the background.

Up and over. Malcolm Finlayson clears his lines during a sun-splashed Wolves victory away to Birmingham City. In five visits to St Andrew's in successive seasons from 1957-58, Finlayson and his team-mates were triumphant against their near-neighbours.

Me and my friends! 'Keeper Finlayson finds no shortage of backers in his kingdom. The Scot, signed from Millwall and later to become a successful businessman linked with buying Wolves, played more than 200 senior games for the club, winning two League championship medals and an FA Cup winners' medal.

Wolves in the early 1960s. Back row (left to right): Kirkham, Gerry Harris, Farmer, Davies, Gardiner (trainer), Finlayson, Thomson, Knighton, Showell. Middle row: Goodwin, Slater, Flowers, Cullis (manager), Crowe, Wharton, Broadbent. Front row: McParland, Murray, Durandt.

Malcolm Finlayson is beaten by a shot at Bolton, but the ball was kicked off the line. Gerry Harris is the grounded Wolves player tackling home forward Doug Holden.

Ted Farmer leads an attack on the Tottenham goal at Molineux in 1961. Spurs won 4-0 to make it 11 successive wins at the start of the season, a First Division record, on their way to completing the Double.

Wolves playing staff line up in 1962.

What a start to 1962-63! Wolves beat Manchester City 8-1 at Molineux. Bert Trautmann is grounded as Ted Farmer celebrates a goal by Terry Wharton (right).

January 27, 1962. Wolves v Albion in a fourth-round FA Cup tie at Molineux, with visiting Bobby Robson and Stan Jones the airborne duo flanking Jimmy Murray. The Albion number-two (left) is Wolverhampton-born Don Howe.

March 27, 1965. Fred Davies foils Alan Gilzean of Spurs at White Hart Lane. John Kirkham keeps a watching brief. Kirkham scored one of Wolves' four goals that day — but Tottenham hit seven and Wolves were on their way down to Division Two.

Playing staff, August 1964. It turned out to be Stan Cullis's last pre-season photo call as he was sacked after the team's poor start to the season. Back row (left to right): Roberts, Broadbent, Kirkham, Farmer, George Palmer (physiotherapist), Gerry Harris, John Harris, Woodruff, Goodwin, Woodfield. Third row: Le Flem, Knighton, Davies, Knight, Barron, Galley, Crawford, Showell, Ford. Seated: Crowe, Wharton, C.Thompson, Flowers, Cullis, Thomson, Melia, Knowles, Buckley, D.Thompson. On ground: Griffiths, Aggio, Carrick, Barnes, Hall, Farrington, Evans.

Hughie McIlmoyle powers in a header, one of the goals in a 3-0 home win over Sheffield United in the fourth round of the FA Cup at Molineux in February 1966.

Wolves in 1966. Back row (left to right): Knowles, Woodfield, Davies, Hunt, Holsgrove, McLaren, McIlmoyle, Wharton. Seated: Ronnie Allen (manager), Knighton, Hawkins, Joe Wilson, Flowers, Thomson, Wagstaffe, Jack Dowen (trainer). On ground: Bailey, Buckley.

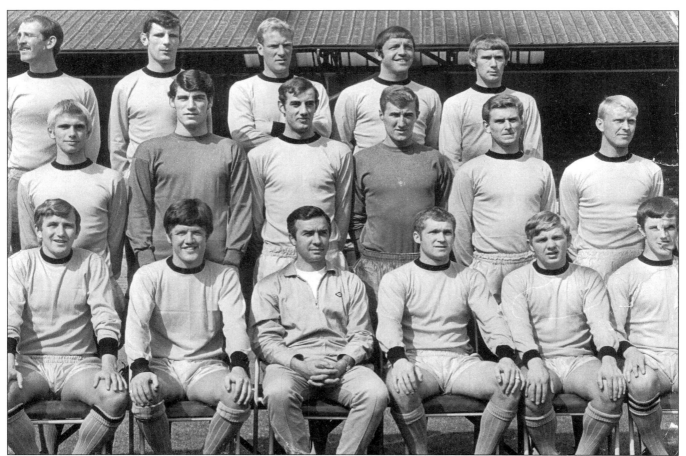

The 1966-67 side who finished second in Division Two. Back row (left to right): Burnside, Woodfield, Flowers, Hunt, Wagstaffe. Middle row: Evans, Parkes, Holsgrove, Davies, Thomson, Hawkins. Front row: Les Wilson, Knowles, Ronnie Allen (manager), Wharton, Buckley, Taylor.

Wolves fans invade the pitch after promotion from the Second Division had been clinched in 1967. Manager Ronnie Allen is about to address them from the directors' box.

August 1971 line-up. Back row (left to right). Curran, Lutton, Oldfield, Munro, Parkes, Woodfield, Hegan. Middle row: Les Wilson, Shaw, Walker, Gould, Richards, McAlle, Hibbitt, Sammy Chung (trainer). Front row: Dougan, Wagstaffe, O'Grady, Bailey, McCalliog, Taylor, Parkin.

Derek Dougan raises his hands after scoring against Leeds in May 1972. Paul Reaney and David Harvey are the crestfallen Leeds players. Wolves won 2-1 to prevent Leeds, who had already won the Cup, from completing the Double.

Disbelief for Leeds' players as they troop off at the end of the 2-1 defeat at Wolves that denied them the League championship in May, 1972. Goals by Frank Munro and Derek Dougan in front of a 53,379 crowd frustrated the Yorkshiremen, who were looking to complete a famous Double after winning the FA Cup two days earlier.

Wolves at Wembley — Part 4

1974 League Cup Final

Wolves 2
Manchester City 1

March 2, 1974. The Football League Cup Final. Frank Munro on the attack, heading for goal as Manchester City's Colin Bell and Mike Doyle sandwich Derek Dougan.

Kenny Hibbitt fires Wolves into the lead against Manchester City at Wembley.

Colin Bell beats Gary Pierce to equalise.

City 'keeper Keith Macrae can't prevent John Richards (number-nine) hitting the winner at Wembley.

Parading the Cup around Wembley after the 2-1 win. Nearest the camera is John McAlle, followed by Barry Powell, Kenny Hibbitt and, with the trophy, Alan Sunderland and Geoff Palmer, then Gary Pierce.

Mike Bailey lets the Cup go to his head.

Wolves show the trophy to their fans.

Home with the Cup. *Left:* Kenny Hibbitt and John Richards with the League Cup on the Town Hall balcony. *Right:* Mike Bailey on the coach as the team make a triumphal tour of Wolverhampton.

Wolves Overseas

Wolves in Russia. Billy Wright gets a bouquet of flowers from Spartak skipper Igor Netto before the game on Sunday, August 7, 1955.

Bert Williams in flying action against Spartak in Moscow.

Dennis Wilshaw, leads an attack on the Dynamo goal on Friday, August 12, 1955. Wolves lost 3-2 with Wilshaw scoring both goals. 1955 was a vintage year for Wilshaw. In April he had become the only man to hit four goals in an England-Scotland full international. He did so in the 7-2 win at Wembley.

The goal that silenced the partisan Italians. Kenny Hibbitt raises his arm to salute Jim McAlliog's volleyed equaliser in the away leg of Wolves' UEFA Cup quarter-final against Juventus in March 1972. Wolves won the second leg 2-1 and went on to reach the Final before losing in anti-climax to Tottenham.

UEFA Cup quarter-final first leg against Juventus in Turin. On the subs' bench are Eastoe, Arnold, Daley, Sunderland and Curran.

Juventus goalkeeper Piloni foils Kenny Hibbitt in the first leg of the UEFA Cup quarter-final in March 1972.

Alan Sunderland watches Mike Bailey's shot go in for the lone Wolves goal against Porto.

September 1974. UEFA Cup round 1. The Porto 'keeper dives to cut out a John Farley cross as Derek Dougan lurks. Wolves lost 4-1.

Wolves in the 1970s

Leeds' revenge! John McAlle and Phil Parkes watch an effort fly just wide of the Wolves post in the 1973 FA Cup semi-final, with Mick Jones and Billy Bremner in close attendance. But Wolves were unable to prevent the sort of last-four heartache they were to become used to over the next few years, this 1-0 defeat at Maine Road being followed by knockouts against Arsenal and Tottenham at the same stage in 1979 and 1981 respectively.

November 1975. Wolves win the national Five-a-Side Cup at the Empire Pool, Wembley. Left to right are Willie Carr, Gary Pierce, John McAlle, Mike Bailey, coach Sammy Chung, Kenny Hibbitt and Alan Sunderland.

Wolves retain the national five-a-side trophy in 1976, the first team to do so. Back row (left to right): Willie Carr, Gary Pierce, Steve Daley, Kenny Hibbitt. Front row: Alan Sunderland and Martin Patching.

The team who won the Second Division in 1976-77 with Sammy Chung the manager.

The club celebrated their centenary in 1977. To mark the occasion they were presented with an illuminated address by the FA. Left to right are Bob Lord (FA vice-president), Wolves chairman Harry Marshall, former FIFA president Sir Stanley Rous and FA chairman Harold Thompson.

Ready for a new season in July 1978. Back row (left to right): Kevin Walters (physiotherapist), Hazell, Daley, Brazier, Pierce, Bradshaw, Berry, Richards, Hibbitt, Palmer, Brian Owen (trainer). Middle row: Wayne Clarke, McAlle, Daniel, Sammy Chung (manager), Rafferty, Bell, Parkin. On ground: Paul Moss, Fleming, Arkwright, Todd, Black, Carr, Jimmy Kelly, Eves.

Wolves v Chelsea in April 1978. Bob Hazell leaps to avoid a tackle from Micky Droy.

Dramatic action from John McAlle, one of the stalwarts of the 1970s side, as he blocks a West Ham shot.

Another FA Cup semi-final. This is the Villa Park version against Arsenal in 1979 as John Richards' feat in out-jumping the Gunners' David O'Leary provides a rare moment of hope for Wolves.

February 1980. League Cup semi-final second leg. Mel Eves celebrates his goal in a 3-1 win over Swindon which clinched the Wembley date.

John Richards slots in his
second in the League Cup
semi-final clash with
Swindon as Andy Gray raises
an arm.

After the win over
Swindon at Molineux,
Kenny Hibbitt is chaired off
by jubilant fans.

A fan adds his congratulations to Derek Parkin following the 1980 League Cup semi-final victory.

Daniel, Gray and Eves open the champagne in the dressing-room after the 1980 League Cup semi-final win.

Wolves at Wembley — Part 5

1980 League Cup Final

Wolves 1
Nottingham Forest 0

League Cup Final 1980. Goalkeeper Paul Bradshaw watches a Nottingham Forest effort go wide as George Berry looks on. Grounded are Forest's Trevor Francis and Wolves' Derek Parkin.

Wolves' skipper Emlyn Hughes heads clear.

Manager John Barnwell says well done to John Richards after the 1980 League Cup Final.

A happy Wembley group after the 1-0 defeat of Nottingham Forest.

John McAlle with the trophy as Wolves make a triumphal return to Wolverhampton.

Manager John Barnwell's turn to let the happy supporters see the trophy.

Assistant manager Richie Barker shows the Cup to the fans.

King John the Sharpshooter

Top, right: One of the all-time Molineux heroes, John Richards signs autographs outside the ground in 1981.

Top, left: Sharp-shooters — John Richards and Derek Dougan, the deadly duo who aimed to gun down opponents in the 1970s.

Left: King John at home with wife Pam sporting a couple of his England caps. Although he won several at Under-23 level, he was, much to the disgust of his adoring fans, awarded only one full cap.

Success never really went to the head of John Richards — but the League Cup did on this occasion as he and Kenny Hibbitt celebrated at the London Hilton following the 1974 Wembley victory over Manchester City.

John Richards, the club's record goalscorer in the years BB (Before Bull), with a player of the season trophy.

Two magnificent former Wolves goalscorers in nostalgic mood. John Richards (194 goals for the club) and the late Billy Hartill (170 between 1929 and 1935).

Scoring goals — it's simple. That's what the gesture from John Richards would seem to imply after Crystal Palace 'keeper Paul Barron had been beaten by him in March 1982.

Legends turned out for Richards's testimonial game against Moscow Dynamo, with England World Cup '66 hero Bobby Charlton and Russian goalkeeping great Lev Yashin there to wish him well.

Bridging the generations, John Richards and pre-war star Tom Galley get together. Galley lives in Cannock where Richards is now a leisure services chief with the local council.

Derek Parkin – Record Holder

Derek Parkin made a record number of appearances for Wolves and was a firm favourite with the fans. He was typically committed in his testimonial game against a Midland All-Star XI in November 1979 as Cyrille Regis and Emlyn Hughes look on.

Wolves' record appearance holder Derek Parkin was also a penalty expert as he shows here against South-ampton's Eric Martin at Molineux with a spot-kick that was twice taken.

Derek Parkin looks the best bet in this race for the ball with Trevor Francis during the 1980 League Cup Final against Nottingham Forest at Wembley.

More than 7,000 fans turned up on a cold November night to wish Parkin, hero of 510 League and Cup games for the club, all the best. Albion skipper John Wile leads the applause as Parkin takes the field.

The 1980s and '90s —Darkness to Light

Steve Archibald celebrates his goal for Spurs at Hillsborough in the 1981 FA Cup semi-final, much to the despair of Derek Parkin, Paul Bradshaw, George Berry, John McAlle and Emlyn Hughes. Wolves, with the help of a last-gasp penalty, drew this game but crashed in the replay at Highbury.

Beginning of the end as Garth Crooks leaps above Geoff Palmer to head Spurs into an 11th-minute lead in the 1981 Highbury semi-final replay they won 3-0.

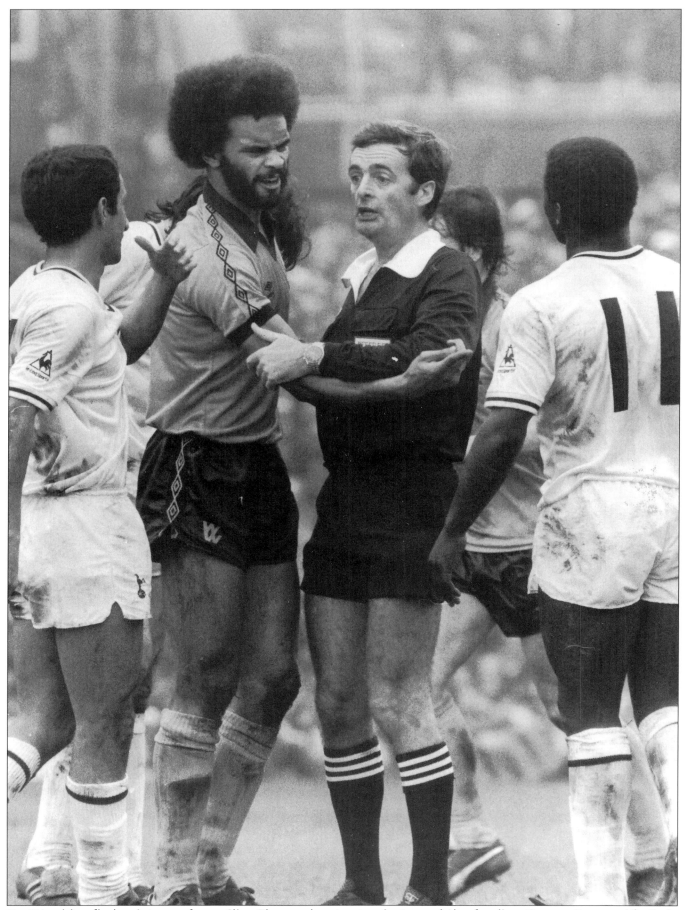

Pre-Wembley flashpoint as referee Clive Thomas has to step in to cool the feuding George Berry, with Ossie Ardiles and Garth Crooks also making their point in the Wolves v Tottenham semi-final.

Ready for the 1980-81 season. Back row (left to right): Brian Garvey (reserve-team coach), Black, Fleming, Atkinson, Coy, Cutler, Hollifield, Butler, Ian Ross (coach). Standing: John Malam (physiotherapist), Jack Taylor (commercial manager), Humphrey, Craig Moss, Matthews, Kearns, Bradshaw, Berry, Brazier, Palmer, Hibbitt, John Jarman (youth development officer). Seated: John Barnwell (manager), Villazan, McAlle, Eves, Daniel, Carr, Hughes, Richards, Parkin, Clarke, Gray, Thomas, Richie Barker (assistant manager). On ground: Rudge, Robotham, Kernan, Pender, Sparrock.

March 1981. Andy Gray heads Wolves in front in the FA Cup sixth-round tie with Middlesbrough at Ayresome Park. 'Boro earned a draw but Wolves won the replay 3-1.

May 1983. Wolves celebrate a quick return to the First Division as (left to right) Gordon Smith, Alan Dodd, David Wintersgill and John Pender greet the fans from the directors' box. Promotion should have been the start of a revival — little did those present know but the worst years in the club's history were about to start.

Getting in trim in Majorca as locals join in are Gordon Smith, Ken Hibbitt and Mel Eves.

Hoping for a good season back in Division One as boss Graham Hawkins turns cameraman, are: Back row (left to right) Humphrey, Coy, Burridge, Eves, Daniel, Matthews. Front row: Pender, Livingstone, Butler, Palmer, Wintersgill, Clarke, Jim Barron (assistant manager). Alas Wolves finished bottom, winning only six League games and the slide had begun.

The 1983-84 squad. Back row (left to right): Daniel, Dodd, Humphrey, Flowers, Bradshaw, Burridge, Pender, Atkinson, Mike Bennett. Standing: Frank Upton (youth coach), Rudge, Towner, Eves, Kellock, Gray, Hibbitt, Clarke, Watkiss, Matthews, Denis Conyard (physiotherapist). Seated: Graham Hawkins (manager), Jackson, Coy, Paul Butler, Palmer, Cartwright, Livingstone, Smith, Jim Barron (assistant manager). On ground: Croke, Rodger, Bayly, Steve Thomas, Wintersgill, Ryan, Dougherty, Bromley.

So this is how bad things became! Empty seats are to be seen everywhere as Wolves labour to a 0-0 draw with Portsmouth in 1984-85 during the second of their three successive relegation seasons. Peter Eastoe tussles here with Noel Blake in front of a paltry attendance of 7,985.

Alan Ainscow looks pretty pleased after scoring against Wimbledon in a 1-1 Division Two draw at Plough Lane. Sadly, Division Three was just a few games away. The number-nine is Mark Buckland.

August 1986. Getting ready for an unwelcome bit of club history — their first season in the Fourth Division. Back row (left to right): Lockhart, Neil Edwards, Barrett, Dean Edwards, Bartram, Turley, Mutch, Stoutt. Standing: Palmer, Hellin, Barnes, Oldroyd, Zelem, Nicky Clarke, Eli, Holmes, Streete, Ryan, Eddie Edwards (physiotherapist). Seated: Wright, Purdie, Dougherty, Brian Little (acting manager), Heywood, Wood, Forman.

Wolves take the field against Burnley at Wembley in the 1988 Sherpa Van Trophy Final.

The 1988 line-up. Back row (left to right): Bull, Nicky Clarke, Bellamy, Streete, Kendall, Venus, Robertson, Mutch. Standing: Paul Darby (physiotherapist), Dennison, Robinson, Downing, Robert Kelly, Chard, Barry Powell (coach). Seated: Vaughan, Gooding, Graham Turner (manager), Thompson, Tom Bennett.

Manager Graham Turner and his greatest buy Steve Bull, after the Third Division title had been clinched against Sheffield United.

Still in the swing. Ron Flowers, one of the golden greats of Wolves' 1950s halcyon days and capped 49 times by England, captured on the golf course in more recent years.

Stars who helped Wolves to three Football League titles in the 1950s met again when the Former Players Association had their inaugural meeting at the *Express & Star* Sports Club. Back row (left to right): Joe Gardiner (trainer during those halcyon days), Ron Flowers, Malcolm Finlayson, Bill Slater. Front: George Showell, Norman Deeley, Eddie Clamp and Gerry Harris.

And this is my top table. New Wolves owner Sir Jack Hayward introduces his directors and senior management staff on the day he bought the club in May 1990. Left to right: Keith Pearson, John Harris, Jack Harris (then chairman), Sir Jack, Jonathan Hayward, Billy Wright, Graham Turner.

Jonathan Hayward, Billy Wright and Sir Jack Hayward pictured on the Molineux pitch just after the club changed hands in 1990.

The thin blue line. Police search for booby-trap devices in the Molineux pitch during a bizarre weekend in May 1992, when saboteurs twice struck at the stadium.

Face in the crowd. Sir Jack, always a man of the people, especially Wolverhampton people.

The partly burned-out Waterloo Road Stand provides an unusual backcloth on the final day of the 1991-92 season as Mark Burke gets airborne during Middlesbrough's promotion-clinching 2-1 win over Wolves.

Those Fantastic Wolves Fans

Players join in the community singing from the tunnel area before a match at Molineux in decades gone by.

Some things never change. The fashions may be of a bygone age, but the spirit of FA Cup Final day is much the same. These Wolves fans are Wembley-bound for the 1939 showdown against Portsmouth.

Fans queuing for tickets for the 1942 two-legged Wartime League Cup Final between Wolves and Sunderland.

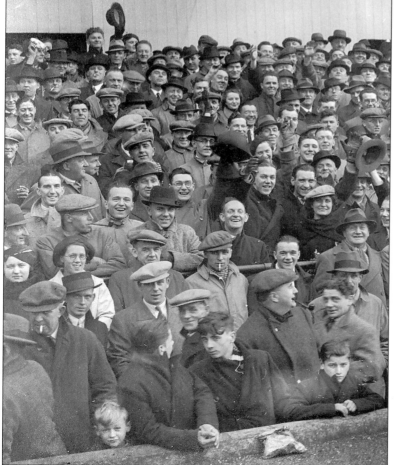

Hats, happy faces and a typically packed Molineux of yesteryear.

Wolves fans at Wembley before the 1980 League Cup Final.

Supporters from Stafford and Rugeley were among the early arrivals at Wembley in 1980 for the League Cup Final against Nottingham Forest.

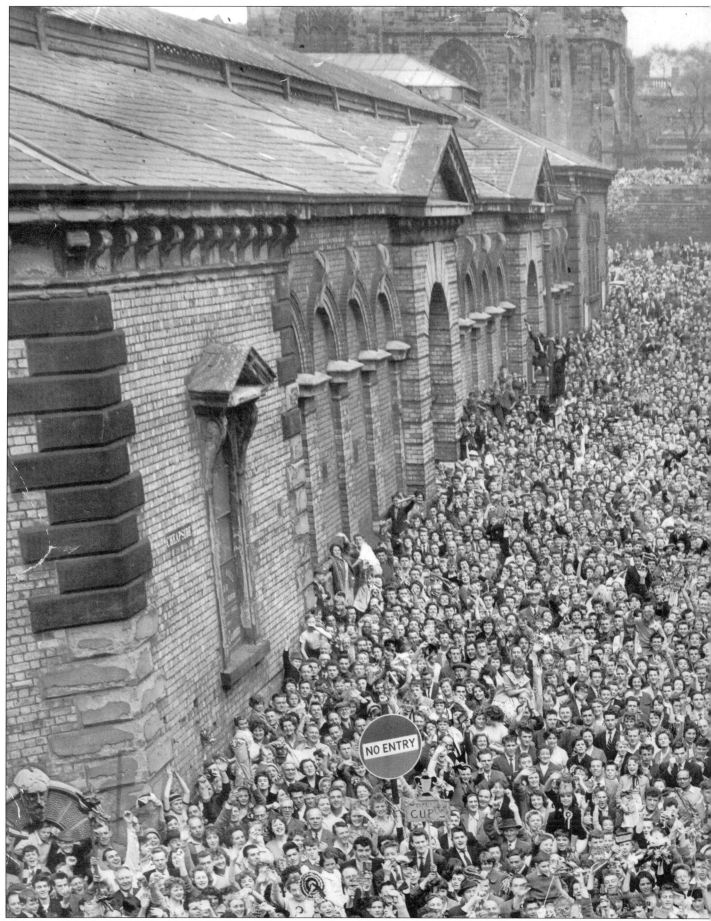

The crowd in front of the Town Hall and alongside the old, much-lamented Market Hall, welcome home the Cup

winners.

Andy's Head Is Deadly says the banner held by these fans before the 1980 League Cup Final. They almost got it right — Gray scored the only goal of the game, but with his foot.

Before the game against Stoke at Molineux a week after the Wembley win over Forest, Ken Hibbitt and Peter Daniel perform a lap of honour with the trophy. The pair were not playing against Stoke because of injuries.

Days of protest. The message is clear from the fans and supporters' club chairman Albert Bates.

TV personality David Coleman, a man with a soft spot for Wolverhampton Wanderers, chairs the Civic Hall crisis meeting organised with the help of the *Express & Star* in the dark days of the 1980s. Left is the PFA's Brendon Batson and next to him, Keith Parker, then editor of the newspaper.

This pitch invasion was at Torquay in November 1986. However, Wolves were cleared by an FA disciplinary committee of any responsibility for the trouble caused by a minority of their supporters.

Queuing at Molineux, for tickets for the 1988 Sherpa Van Trophy Final against Burnley at Wembley.

Fans who had queued all night in a bid to get tickets for the 1987 Fourth Division Play-off clash with Aldershot.

Taking goals to Newcastle. The exodus of Wolves fans on New Year's Day 1990 for the game at St James' Park. Steve Bull made the trip worthwhile, scoring all his side's goals in a 4-1 win.

Have Wheels, Will Travel

Wolves on a visit to Ireland with Bill Crook and Jesse Pye enjoying a leisurely form of transport.

Off to Ireland by boat in the mid-1930s, with Bryn Jones, Joe Gardiner, Stan Cullis and Tom Galley among those aboard.

Wolves on their travels in the late 1930s with Stan Cullis and Joe Gardiner centre of the group.

Letting the train take the strain. Wolves' players pictured on the platform as they head for an away game in the mid-1930s.

A good-luck send-off for Bryn Jones (left) and Tom Smalley from friendly staff at Wolverhampton's Low Level station.

Striding out on match-day. From left: Dennis Westcott, Alex McIntosh, Dickie Dorsett and manager Major Frank Buckley.

'Training' again. The Wolves contingent, including pre-war star Frank Taylor (without hat) and Stan Cullis (turning, in background), step off the platform *en route* for an away game.

Shouting from the bus-top! The name of a well-known Wolverhampton coach company is clearly on display as Billy Wright and his victorious team-mates emerge from the town's Low Level railway station during their triumphant homecoming after the 1949 FA Cup Final win over Leicester City.

FA Cup 1960. Bill Slater and Gerry Harris hold the Cup as the coach takes the winning team through the town centre.

Wolves on their travels again — to Lokomotiv Leipzig in the first leg of their second round UEFA Cup tie, in October 1973. Wolves lost 3-0.

Off to the sunshine of Majorca in May 1983. From top of the steps: Matthews, Bradshaw, Eves, Rudge, Cartwright, Humphrey, Pender. Waiting to join the rest are (left to right) physiotherapist Denis Conyard, vice-chairman Doug Hope and assistant manager Jim Barron. The trip was to celebrate promotion back to the First Division.

Something to celebrate after the bleak years — fans welcome home the side who beat Burnley 2-0 to win the Sherpa Van Trophy at Wembley in 1988.

It's All In The Training

Training in front of the Waterloo Road Stand in the late-1920s.

Ready for training at Molineux in the late-1930s.

A Wolves group in training in the 1930s. Goalkeeper Alf Tootill is second left and Billy Hartill fifth left.

Mike Bailey and Derek Dougan lead a training stint at Worthing before the Football League Cup Final of 1974. Behind Dougan is Gary Pierce who got into the team at Wembley on his birthday. Following them are Steve Daley, Derek Parkin and Geoff Palmer.

That Magical Place Called Molineux

Molineux in 1869 at the time of the South Staffs Fine Arts and Industrial Exhibition.

How Molineux looked around 1905. It was described as 'the classic playing field of the Wolverhampton Wanderers Football Club'.

Kickabout time for two former Wolves directors shortly after World War One. The dressing-rooms, in between the North Bank and Molineux Street Stand, are in the background.

An impressive gathering of latter-day dignitaries as the new Waterloo Road Stand is officially opened on September 12, 1925, by Football League president Mr J.McKenna. Wolves marked the happy event with a 4-1 League victory at home to Portsmouth.

It may not be obvious apart from the town name on the advertising board, but this IS Molineux.

Wolves 0 Hull 1 in an FA Cup third-round match in 1925. A packed South Bank as ever — and, in those days, open to the elements.

Supporters packed into the North Bank for the 4-1 home win over Portsmouth in September 1925 — the day the Waterloo Road Stand was opened. Note the old 'Cow Shed' structure.

After the storm had struck. Bystanders survey the damage caused by a Sunday night gale to the Molineux Street stand in 1925. The structure was that previously used as the Waterloo Road Stand until its rebuilding in 1925. The wreckage blocked the road for several hours.

The new Waterloo Road Stand after its opening in 1925. Note the tramlines.

And how it looked further up towards the South Bank.

146 FT.

96 FT.

How they measured up: this view from the old Park Road looking up Molineux Street towards Wolverhampton town centre shows the height the pylons were in 1957 (96ft), with an artist's impression of how high they were planned to become (146ft).

A famous addition to the Wolverhampton skyline. Molineux's floodlight pylons photographed during their installation in the 1950s. Towering above the cars of the day, they also dwarf the South Bank roof and the Fox Inn, the latter still part of the mid-1990s landscape.

Above: How Molineux looked for decades from Waterloo Road.

Right: Those were the days. £2 for a place on the North Bank, a sign that went when the stand was demolished to make way for the Stan Cullis Stand.

Below: With the Waterloo Road stand disused, Wolverhampton Council decide that in July 1987 corrugated iron sheeting must be taken down as a safety measure.

The North Bank in decay and soon to be replaced by the Stan Cullis Stand.

Molineux before its dramatic redevelopment with the Waterloo Road and North Bank stands dwarfed by the John Ireland Stand.

A crane reaches out towards a floodlit pylon on the North Bank. The pylons that went to make way for the new Molineux were not the ones that had lit the famous wins over Honved and Spartak. Those went in the late 1950s.

Another view of the old North Bank, which was still known as the Cow Shed End, even though the shed-like stand that gave it its name had been demolished before the war.

Work begins on the new ground. With the North Bank gone, the Stan Cullis Stand shell is erected.

The Stan Cullis Stand under construction.

The dream that became reality. This artist's impression of Molineux's main entrance and frontage, based on the work of the Alan Cotterell Partnership, soon materialised in bricks and mortar. The structure was there in all its glory by the middle of 1993.

Aerial view of the magnificent 'new' stadium, redeveloped on three sides between 1991 and 1993 and financed by the generosity of the Hayward family. Estimates in 1996 put the cost of the work, which also included refurbishment of the existing John Ireland Stand, at more than £20m.

This and That

The day Wolves crashed out of the FA Cup in more ways than one. When they lost to Bournemouth in the fourth round. Reg Cutler not only scored the only goal of the game, he also ended up in the net and snapped the goal post.

Wembley here we come! Norman Deeley hits home the only goal of the 1960 semi-final against Villa at The Hawthorns.

Peter Broadbent, without a doubt, the hub of the great team of the late 1950s, with the Football League championship trophy in 1954. It was the first such triumph in Wolves' history.

Twenty-one's the number. Ted Farmer scores against Everton at Molineux on January 21, 1962, on his 21st birthday. It was his 21st game for the first team — and his 21st goal.

No play today. Wolves general manager Jack Howley surveys a wintry scene on the day all the club's matches were wiped out by the snow on December 9, 1967.

Top left: Peter Knowles on the ball and about to torment another opposing defence. *Top right:* The messages outside the ground were clear, but Knowles had made up his mind. *Above:* In scoring against Fulham in April 1964 he collided with goalkeeper Tony Macedo and ended up prone on the pitch.

A sad day for fans as Peter Knowles bids farewell after his final game for the club, against Nottingham Forest in September 1969, Knowles left because he felt he could not be a full-time footballer and be true to his religion as a Jehovah's Witness. Apart from the occasional testimonial game, Knowles has not played since and says his decision was undoubtedly the right one.

A young supporter wipes away a tear as Knowles leaves the ground following the match.

Before Wolves played Crystal Palace on September 8, 1979, there was other business to undertake – the little matter of manager John Barnwell clinching the record signing of Andy Gray from Aston Villa. The fee? – roughly one-tenth of a Shearer.

Half-backs all. Four men who were the engine room of the 1950s team, get together at the inaugural meeting of the Former Player Association. Left to right are Ron Flowers, Bill Slater, Eddie Clamp and Billy Wright. In four successive internationals in 1958, Clamp, Wright and Slater formed the England half-back line. To illustrate the club's strength in this position, when the England selectors dropped Slater, they chose Flowers to replace him.

The days of the South Bank are almost at an end. The terrace which once held 30,000 fans, was demolished to make way for the Jack Harris Stand. Club president Sir Jack Hayward could not resist being among the fans for the historic farewell to the last remaining standing area at Molineux during the defeat of Millwall in May 1993.

A Major event in Wolverhampton — when the Prime Minister paid a visit, he met record-breaking striker Steve Bull, who showed him one of the club's famous gold shirts. Behind Bull is Wolves director Billy Wright while manager Graham Turner is on the right.

It had to happen, a Bull in a china shop! The star man was paying a visit to the china department at Beattie's store in Wolverhampton.

Bully for England. The goalscoring legend in action for England 'B' against Italy at Brighton in November 1989.

To mark the start of work on the Billy Wright Stand, it was decided to bury a time capsule which will be opened again in 2014, the 125th anniversary of Wolves' first game at the ground. Among items in the capsule were the two FA Cup Final editions of the *Sporting Star*, a *Wolverhampton Chronicle* report of the first game played at Molineux, Steve Bull's boots, one of Billy Wright's England caps and an 1871 picture showing Molineux grounds before they became the club's home. Burying the capsule are Wright, Ann Simmons of the building contractors McAlpine, club president Sir Jack Hayward, McAlpine managing director Stewart Tilley and Graham Rowley, an *Express & Star* reader who won a competition to decide what should go in the capsule.

Subscribers

Mrs Mary Abbiss
Carl Abbott
Albert Abbotts
Anwar Ahmed
R L Allden
C N Allen
Colin Allen
Simon Andersen
David Anderson
Mr W A Anderson
A S Andrews
Brian S Andrews
Mr J Antcliffe
E S Aris
R V and P M Aris
Peter John Armfield
Matthew Armitage
Anthony John Armstrong
D W J Arnold
S D Asbury
Mr T Asbury
Mr J Ash
Michael Ashmore
P Neil Ashton
Martin N Astley
Stephen Aston
D J Aulton
Dennis Austin

Malcolm S Babb
P R Bagley
Peter Bagley
Nigel Bagnall
Barry J Bailey
David Bailey
Michael F Bailey
M N Bailey
David Baker
David Baker
Ross Baker
W Baker
Stephen Baker
John Ball
Melvyn Ballard
Nick Balmforth
A Banham
Mr and Mrs D Banks
Stu Banks
Mr J D Barlow

Mr A E Barnes
Dennis Barnes
John Barnes
David R Barnett
Mr George Peter Barnett
S A Barnett
G A Barnfield
Lee Barnsley
Lloyd R Baron
Bill Barratt
G G Barratt
P Barrett
Philip Barron
S Bartlett
Brian Barwise
Mr A Bates, Australia
Don Bates
Ian Bates
Muriel and Albert Bates
P K Bates
Simon Battersby
Matthew J Baugh
Simon Bayley
George Baylis
Leslie Bayliss
Mr R Beaman
G J Beaumont
Mrs B Beckley
Brian Bellingham
Brian Bendall
C Bennett
David Bennett
Paul Bennett
W F Bennett
Mr J H Benson
Wayne Bentley
Tony Bess
Mr F W Bestall
Andrew Bickley
Mr Michael A Bickley
Richard Bickley
Wayne Bigford
Mr E Bill
H Billingsley
Brian Birch
John Birch
Mark Birch
P Birchall
P V Bird

Michael Birkenshaw
Stephen Bishop
Tony, Luke and Adam Bishop
E C Blakemore
Joe Blakesley
Mr R J Blank
R J Blanton
P Bloor
Norman Blunt
Kelvin Boddy
Mark Bodin
H W Bolus
John Bonas
Barry Bond
Simon Bond
M Bonnor
Michael Boucher
Keith Bourne
Martyn Bourne
A Bowater
John Bowden
M Bowdler
Alan Bowen
Mrs M V Bowen
C A Bowyer
P J Boyden
Dr Paul Boyle
James Andrew Boynton
Mr M Bradford
Andrew James Bradley
D C Bradley
John and Owen Bray
D P Brazenall
John Brazier
Clive Breakwell
J Breakwell
M Bremner
W J Brett
J D Brewe
C Brice
Jean Brindley
Mr Roger Brindley
N Brinsdon
Allan Briscoe
Des Brittain
C K Britton
Gavin Brook
Ashley P Brookes
Gordon Brookes
Michael Brooks
Mr Brian E Broome
D M Brotherton
Clifford Brown
Mr David Brown
Gerald Thomas Brown
John Brown

Nicholas Brown
Nick Brown
Stanley Brown
John Buckby
R P Buckerfield
M F Bucknall
Michael Budge
Ivan Bull
Mr F W Bullingham
Mark Nicholas Bullock
Matt Bunn
Anne Burgess née Watkins
Simon Burns
Mr David Paul Burrows
E Burrows
Mr W Burton
Tom Butler
M AP Buttery
David Byfield
Robert Bytheway

R H Caddick
T J Cadman
Carol and Martin Cain
Donald K Camp
M Campbell
Norman James Capes
I Capewell
Adrian Carrington
Colin D Carter
Mrs Frances Cartwright
Rob Cartwright
Gary Carvey
Mark Castle
J Challenger
R Challenger
John Chard
Phillip Cherrington
Roger Cheshire
Phillip John Chew
Victor Roy Chillingsworth
David Chinn
J Chrimes
Mr Dennis Clapham
David Clare
W J Clare
Christopher Clark
David Clarke
Martin Clarke
P J Clarke
James Clews
Rob Clutton
Andrew Cockayne
William Cockbill
Ian Collett
Mr Kenneth Collins

S Cornes
Robert Compston
Mick Conway
Christopher Cook
David Cook
Malcolm Cook
Adrian Cooper
Craig Cooper
J W Cooper
Jean and Len Cooper
John Cooper
Mrs S L Cooper
Gordon Corbett
James Corbett
P I Corby
Leanne Corns
George Cotgrave
C L Cottam
Dave Cotterill
Bob Cowern
Christopher D Cox
David Cox
Derek Cox
Mildred Cox
O M Cox
Thomas Cox
Peter Craddock
Raymond Craggs
John A Crawford
Ian S Creaser
John Creed
L Cresswell
John A Cross
Rosemary Crump
Steve Crumpton
Robert Cubbon
Mr L B Custance

Timothy Dakley
R S Dando
John E Dannatt
Kieran Darby
Peter J Darby
Geoffrey Darter
Mr Davies
A W Davies
J M Davies
Keith Davies
Margaret Davies
Nigel and Harry Davies
Paul Davies
R H Davies
Ron Davies
Roy S Davies
S J Davies
T N Davies

Glyn Stanley Davis
Matthew Davis
Neil A Davis
Robert Davis
W B Davis
E J Davison
Chris Daw
Mr John Dawkins
Miss B Dawson
Mr Andrew Deakin
Tony Deakin
J T Dean
Barry Deeming
Mrs G Degg
Alexander Dent
Merv Denton
Michael Deveney
Mark Dewson
Antony J Dicken
John Dicken
Philip Dicken
Robert Dicken
I C Dickins
Paul, Jonathan and Darren Dickens
M J Dilland
M R P Dodd
S L Dodd
Michael Doherty
Jack Douglass
Richard Downs
Mr John Doyle
Dean Draisey
Mr and Mrs B L Drew (Canada)
L I Dudley
Teresa B Dudley
Gerard Duffy
Andrew Robert Dugmore
D Dungar
Wilfrid J Dunn
Mrs D Dunning
Angus Dunphy
Mitchell Dutton
George Duttongolds
Mr T W Dyke
Paul Dyson

Colin Eagle
Frank Eagle
Simon Earp
Jon Ebert
C Eccleston
J A Edge
Mr P Edgerton
Helen Edgington
A H Edwards
J M Edwards

John Edwards
Neil Geoffrey Edwards
Nick Edwards
Robert Edwards
Mr Jason Elbro
Howard Elkin
Mrs J E Ellis
Glyn O Ellis
P J Elson
David Emery
Mrs L England
Steve English
Rex Everall
David T Evans
E Evans
Frederick Evans
Ian Evans
Mr M J Evans
Mr Mark N Evans
Mrs R C Evans
Ray Evans
E Everett
John A Everitt

Mr D Facer
Keith Farley
David Farmer
Martin Farmer
Mr J T Farr
M A Fasey
Mr B J Faulkner
Ian D Favill
John E Favill
Stephen J Favill
Robert Feder
Christopher Steven Fellows
J F Fellows
Ron Fellows
S Fellows
Paul Ferguson
William H Fern
Angela Field
Paul Fielding-Fox
Tony Filipski
G C Flavell
Gordon Flavell
M S Flavell
Simon Flavell
W Fleet
T W Fletcher
David James Foley
R W Ford
Michael P Forde
Bill and Enda Forrest (Canada)
John Foster
Laurence Foster

Richard Foster
Denis G Foulkes
Eric W Foulkes
J and K Fownes
J A Francis
Mr J A Fraser
Luke Fraser
Roy Fuchco
L W Fullelove
G P Fuller
E Fullwood
Paul Furber

P G
Mr G H Gabb
C A Galleymore
Mr William Galliers
B W Gamston
David Gandy
Mrs G Gandy
Roy Garner
Mr S R Garner
Dave Garratt
Lee Gilchrist
(South London Harriers) Mr F D Gilson
J W Glassey
Daniel Guy Glaze
Mrs Edna Glaze
Gwladys Glazzard
John Glen
Mr Keith Gliest
Max Godridge
Jack Godwin
John Golding
M C Goldsmith
R W J Goodall
Stephen Goodey
Steve Gower
Mrs C Graham
Mr A W Grainger
C Grainger
Colin Gray
David Green
Geoffrey Green
John B Green
R Green
Richard Green
Robert H Green
Roger Green
Ron Green
John Gregory
Robin Gregory
Peter Greybanks
Alan Griffiths
Barry Griffiths
Mr Bert Griffiths

G Griffiths
David T Grice
Andrew Griggs
Marc Groves
Peter D Groves
Mrs E Guest
Hannah Gunter
Darron Guttery
Jason Guy
John Guy

Paul and Brian Hackitt
C D Haddon
Roy Hadley
Michael John Hailey
Peter Hailey
I F Hale
Niel Craig Hale
Mr R A Hale
Roger K Halfpenny
Adrian Hallam
Christopher Hallam
M S Halsall
Christopher Hammond
David Hammonds
John Hammonds
M Hampton
Robert Hancock
Peter Hand
Jim and Sue Handley
W Ronald Hands
Ruston Handy
Thomas R Handy
M Hannaford
P A Hardwicke
Mr Terry Hargrove
C Harper
David Harper
G K Harper
Graham Harridence
C Harriman
David L Harriman
Ian W Harriman
Mr M G Harriman
Richard Harrington
Mrs Brenda Harris
E Harris
G E Harris
James Harris
R A Harris
T Harris
G Harrison
J Harrison
Ken Harrison
Steve Harrold
Jonathan Hart

Chris Haseley
Les Hatton
Bernard Haw
Neil Hawkins
R M Hawkins
Andy Haycock
Joan Hayfield
David Haytree
Mr John Hayward
Steven Hazeldine
Mr D Head
Mark Healey
D M Hedges
Raymond George Hendy
E Heritage
Mrs R A Heseltine
Michael Hespley
A J Hewitt
Mrs D Hewitt
Ray Hewitt
Roy Hewitt
James Hewson
Stephen Hibbs
Mark Hickman
William John Hickman
A R Hill-Harding
Christopher I Hill
Eric Hill
Mr G E Hill
Mr Trevor Hill
S T C Hines
A F Hingley
Mrs P Hinks
A J Hipwell
Mrs J Hipwell
A R Hobbs
P J Hodgkinson
Alan Hodgkiss
Mr B Holden
D N Holding
Mr W Holt
Brett Homer
David Homer
Jason Paul Homer
Geoff Hood
Michael Hood
David Hope
A R Hopkins
Stephen Hopkins
M Horrobin
B M Horstman
Paul Horton
Spencer Fred Horton
Robert A Howe
Christopher Howell
V Howells

Mrs Bessie Huband
Mr John Huband
Neil Hudson
Rex Hudson
David Hughes (South Australia)
William Hughes
David Humphreys
John Humphries
Mr G Hussey
C R Hutchings
Mrs D Hyde

Cecilia D M Iliff
E W Ingram

Donald Jacks
Martin Jacks
Mrs P Jacks
Barbara Jackson
G Jackson
Neil Jackson
Stephen Jackson
A James
A H James
B W James
Laura James
Pamela James
Jeff Jefferies
K M Jeffrey
David Jenkins
G Jenkins
J C Jennings
C Jervis
Dave Jevons
J E Johnson
W Johnson
K Johnston
Mrs A E Jones
A R Jones
Mr Clive Jones
Craig Jones
Edward T Jones
Mr F R Jones
Graham Jones
Glen Jones
Glyn H Jones
H Jones
Helen Victoria Jones
J G Jones
John Jones
Mr K T Jones
Kenneth S Jones
L A J Jones
Mark Jones
Martyn Jones
P N Jones

Mrs Patricia Jones
Rob Jones
Robert F Jones
Tom Jones
Les Jordan
Mr R J Jordan
David Judson

William Kay
Tomas Keefe
Michael Robert Keeley
Clive Keeling
Tom Kelly
Derek Kelsey
Michael Kemp
Norman E Kempson
Ian Kendrick
Roy Kennerley
Matthew Kent
Mr Peter Kent
M E Kettley
Bernard Key
David Key
Alan King
Leslie King
Richard John Kingston
Mrs Elsie Kirkwood
Mr J Kitching
Mr C Knight
Reginald John Trafford Knipe
Mr W J Knowles
Alec Kokinis
Mr David Kyte
Mr P W Kyte

Robert E Lacey
A R Laidler
Nick Lakin
Trevor Lambeth
Patrick Landucci
David Lane
Lee Lane
G E Langford
Peter Langford
Patti Larard
Barry Latham
N Law
Gary Lawley
F M Lawrence
Francis Layzell
Mrs J Lea
Barry F Leadbeater
Andy Leake
Mrs Dora Leek
Anthony Guy Lees
R R Lees

Mark Leighton
S T Leighton
John Lench
Michael Leng
Thomas Lenham
Mr G Lester
Dennis Lewis
W Lewis
Mark David Liddington
Nicholas Ling
Mr A Lippett
Alex Littleford
C A Lloyd
J E Lloyd
John D Lloyd
Matthew Lloyd
C Lockley
David J Lockley
Richard Lockley
Ian M Lones
Alan W Lovatt
John Lovatt
Mr S P Lovell
Mr P Lovell
Stuart Lowbridge
David J Lowe
Peter C Lowe
Colin Loynton
Grenville Lucas

Peter William McCamley
Mark McDaniels
Tom McDermott
Kieran MacDonald
Robert McEwan
Robert McEwan
Mr H A H Macey
Anthony McHale
Brendan McInerney
John D McKenna
Paddy McShane
Sheila B McTaggart
David L Maddocks
Philip Magness
K E Maiden
Clive Male
Tony Mallam
P Mallin
A Mander
Oliver Manley
Charles Manning
Ron Manning
M J Mantripp
Charles W Marritt
L Marsh
Simon Marsh

L M Martin
William Martin
J W Mason
Neil Maton
Reg Maton
Andrew G Matthews
J Maund
Mr H Mawdsley
Mr A R Maxted
Ian Maybury
Brian Meddings
Adrian Mellor
Geoffrey Mellor
Mr S W Mellor
Mark Meredith
Dennis Merrick
Scott Midgley
Norman Miller
Mr Eric J Millington
Eric Millichap
James Millis
Arthur W Mills
Craig Mills
James Mills
R G Millward
B A Mitchell
C J Molineux
Andrew Moore
John Moran
G Morgan
Keith Morgan
Peter Morgan
Peter Morgan
Roydon Morgans
Mr A Morris
Carl Morris
E Morris
E M Morris
John Trevor Morrison
Tony Morroll
Lawrence Muir
Roy Mullard
Mark Murphy

G Narraway
J Nash
Neil
T Newland
Mr K J Newman
Philip and Peter Newton
Mrs B Neylan
D Nicholas
D A Nicholls
Dennis Nicholls
Jean Nicholls
Richard Nicholls

S Nicklin
Mr B Nightingale

Adrian Oakes
Kevin O'Connell
Eric Oldfield
Luke Oliver
Craig O'Mahony
Mr Gordon W Onions
B M Onions
Andy Overton
Geoff Owen
J Owen
Keith Alexander Owen
Richard Owen

John Edward Pace
M Paddock
M F Palmer
T R Palmer
Christopher Pardo
G H Pardoe
T Parkes
Trevor Parkes
Clive Parr
T R Parsons
Mr T Parton
Steven Partridge
G G Passey
Umesh Patel
David A Pauling
K A Paulins
N J R Payton
M Pearce
Nigel Pearce
Mr R G Pearce
Mark Alan Pearse
Brett Pearson
Matthew James Pearson
Michael and Diane Pearson
Robert Pearson
Steven Pearson
James Edward Peate
Carl Peddie
Miss R Pedley
Tom Peet
Mrs L K Pemberton
R C Pendrell
Trevor J Penk
Mr M T Penny
Miss N J Penny
Mr S M Penny
Mr T Penny MBE
Nigel Stuart Perkins
A E Perry
Dean Perry

Mr Robert Perry
Steven Petford
Melvin Phillips
Jonathan Phipps
E J Picken
Les Pickerill
H J Pickering
Mrs J M Pitt
Logan Plant
Mrs S J Plant
Mr Jack Platt
G W Plummer
Ruth Polack
Ronald Ponder
A E Poole
R J Poole
Michael Pote
Mrs C I Pottle
R Potts
Ray Potts
John Pountain
Mark Povey
Andrew Powell
Dr Simon G Powell
Don Poyner
B G Poynton
Mr D Poyner
R J Preece
Eric S Preston
Mrs Freda Preston
Mr Lawrence Preston
Paul Preston
Barry Price
Bill Price
Geoffrey Price
Peter Price
Richard Price
Richard Price
Trevor Price
Michael Priest
M A Pritchard
Mr Alan Proctor
N Prodger
Hannah Prosser
C B Proud
Chris Proudman
Mr D J Pugh

G O Raison
V M Ralphs
John Ransom
Dennis Ray
HH Raybould
W A Rayson
John Reade
A Reaney

Mike Redfern
Ian Redmond
G T Reed
David Rees
Michael Relves
Matthew Revitt
Gordon Reynolds
Kevin P Reynolds
R Rhann
David S Richards
Mr Michael John Richards
Steven M Richards
Phillip Richardson
Mrs H Ridgway
Stuart Rigby
Ian Ritchie
P J Reynolds
T A Robbins
A J Roberts
David Roberts
D J Roberts
Joan Roberts
K M Roberts
R J Roberts
Samuel Roberts
Mr Warren A J Roberts
A R J Robinson
John Alfred Robinson
Robert John Robinson
Damian Roche
Mr David J Roden
Harold Roden
D Rogers
David W Rogers
Ian Rogers
John Rogers
Neil Rogers
David Rollason
Michael Rollason
Thomas Roobottom
Michael Rose
David Rothin
Dennis Rowlands
Arthur Rudge
John F Russell
J Ryley

John Sadler
Keith Sadler
Colin Salter
K Sambrook
M R Sambrooks
Michael F Sampson
E G Sanders
M Saunders
Philip Saunders

Geoffrey Scrivens
Mrs J Scott
John H Searl
Michael Seedhouse
E H Shakespeare
J Geoffrey Shakespeare
Adam Shamma
David Shamma
Ian Shamma
James Sharkey
Diane Sharp
P Sharples
Jeff Shaw
Stephen Shaw
Alistair Shepherd
C Shepherd
Julie and Andrew Shepherd
Arthur John Sherwood
Winifred W E Sherwood
R G Shingler
Graham Shortland
Craig Simmons
Donna Skidmore
Mr G Skidmore
Les and Pearl Skitt
Mr J Skelson
Mr A R Skidmore
David Slape
Doreen Slater
S F Slater
Rob Sloan
Donald Sly
Ian Slym
Christian Smith
Cyril Smith
David Smith
M G Smith
George Smith
J V Smith
John A Smith
Mr John T Smith
Nick Smith
Patrick J Smith
Paul Smith
Peter Smith
Philip Smith
R J Smith
Ralph L Smith
Reg Smith
Stanley Norman Smith
W A Smith
Keith Southall
S J Southey
Karl Spicer
Russell Spinks
Amanda Spittle

H M Springthorpe
Nigel Henry Springthorpe
A R Stafford
Clifford Stanley
R Stanley
Paul Stanton
Denis Stanworth
H J Staples
J P Starkey
John Statham
Klaus Steinborn-Busse
A P Stephenson
John Stevens
Ron Stevens
W Steventon
Steve Stewart
J T F Stimpson
Mr D Stoddart
John Stone
A E Strange
Malcolm Stride
Luke Strong
P A Strother
David Summers
Michael J Sutton
Peter Szyman

John Tandy
Tango From Stourbridge
J E Tanner
Owen Tanner
Roy Tansley
Alan F Taylor "North Carolina"
Brian Taylor
Darrin Taylor
I E Taylor
J & R Taylor
Mr Laurence Taylor
Michael Taylor
Miss S Taylor
Mr and Mrs A Tedd
Christopher Teed
Billy A Terry
Carl Melvyn Thomas
Michael Thomas
Barry Thompson
D J Thompson
Mr M R Thompson
Mr Simon Thompson
Mr P Thornes
R V Timbrell
A F Timmins
Mr John E Timmins
Neil James Timmins
A K Timmis JP
Mark Tipton

Mr A J Tomkins
Graham Tonks
Sarah Tonks
N Towlson
Mr Peter Tranter
Lee Tredwell
Keith Trevor
Margaret Trott
A J Truelove
Clive Tully
Tony Tully
M A Turner
A D Turner
C H Turner
Glenn K Turner
Mr R Turner
Robert Turner
T S Turner
Scott Turley
G O Turvey
Ron Twist

Michael Upton

P A Vingoe
S B Vint

Gerald Wainwright
G P Wakelam
Mr Stuart Wakeley
James Derek Walford
G S Walkeden
Brian Walker
Eddie Walker
G A Walker
H C Walker
R E Walker
Mark Waller
I J Walmsley
Mark Walpole
Ann M Walsh
Neil Walters
Barbara Walton
Gary Ward
Leonard Warrilow
Joe Waterfield
W A Waterfield
Raymond Waters
Mr W Waters
Brian Watkiss
Mrs A Watson
John Watson
Gordon Watton
Mr Jack Watton
Mr W E Watts
Mr A G Webster

William Webster
F J Weedman
M T Welch
Alan Wells
Andrew George Wells
A Wenlock
David John Wenlock
Mr G Wesley
Richard G West
Stanley West (AUS)
D M Westley
Dennis Weston
Mr W G Weston
Carl Westwood
David Westwood
David Westwood
Lawrence Westwood
Neil Westhead
Dean Wheatley
William While
June Whitbread
Irene White
John Thomas White
K White
Neil White
Peter White
William White
Mr Brian Whitehall
Alan Whitehouse
David James Whitehouse
Dennis Whitehouse
Michael Whitehouse
Terry Whittingham
Nigel Wiggin
Gary Wilde
Reg Wilding
Geoff Wilding
Robin Wilding
Nigel Wiley
G Wilkes
Thomas Wilkes
John Wilkins
Michael Wilkinson
Barry Williams
Clifford Williams
Clive Williams
David Williams
G Williams
John Williams
K Williams
M W Williams

P D Williams (Central Library Archives, Wolverhampton)
Phil Williams
Simon J Williams
Mr J Williamson
Mr Richard Willoughby
D Willis
Mr S Wills
J E Wilson
John Wilson
Mark Winmill
Darren Winwood
J Withers
Matt Withington
David Wollam
Ray Wolverson
Robert Wolverson
Carl Wood
David J Wood
M J G Wood
Matthew Wood
Philip L Wood
Martin Woodall
E L Woodberry
Mr J C Wooding
F W Woodsby
Richard Woodward
Jo-Anne Woolaway
L W Woolliscroft
Leonard Wootton
W D Worrall
N Worthington
Roger Worton
Hedley and Jeannie Worwood
Alex Wright
Betty Wright
Kenneth R Wright
Martin Wright
Michael J Wright
Mr R D Wright
Tony Wright
Trevor Wright
W Wright
Terry Wrighton
M C Wyers
Hazel Wyke

Stewart Yapp
John and Dean Yates
Mr C R Yates